ONCE CAUGHT, N

Norman Grubb from the portrait by James E. Seward,
of Cleveland, Ohio

ONCE CAUGHT, NO ESCAPE

MY LIFE STORY

by

Norman Grubb

LONDON
LUTTERWORTH PRESS

First published 1969

7188 1645 5

*Printed in Great Britain by Richard Clay (The Chaucer Press), Ltd.,
Bungay, Suffolk*

CONTENTS

5

CONTENTS

FOREWORD

ANY OF MY CONTEMPORARIES IN THE SERVICE OF CHRIST COULD sit down and write their memoirs for just as good a reason as I. It is only in the last year or two that the thought has even come to me, and I had kept no diaries nor made any preparations through life for doing so. But various friends, especially here in the U.S.A., who had read some of the other books or with whom I had formed links through meetings, began making the suggestion. This headed up in two special friends, John and his wife, Bobbie, Ames, asking me several times over to come and use their Guest House for as long as I like for writing them, in the quiet pinewoods near the home they had recently built in Marion, Alabama.

Finally, I just took this to be the Lord pressing me into doing it, so I went there for November 1967. I was alone, with the large long living-room to pace about in, an electric typewriter provided and a typist for a few days when the first part of the fair copy was ready.

The latter part, of which I finished the revision back home, was very kindly typed by another friend, Mrs. Lydia McClain, whose letters I had used for the last chapter of the book, *God Unlimited*, and which have brought light to so many.

The final fitting up of the manuscript has been in the home which yet another kind friend has for several years given my wife Pauline and myself on her estate on Long Island for a summer vacation—Mrs. Aymar Johnson.

I have naturally written these straight out of my heart and mind from a purely personal point of view, and for that reason it has not been difficult to do, but rather a thrill to me to run back over the stages of my life and trace the abundant grace of God. The Psalmist said rightly, "The Lord *is* good and doeth good." What a mercy to have been "captured" young, and that is why I use this title. Once captured, no escape! You can't, you don't want to, you don't!

I do recognize one thing, however. Through the years you mellow, I suppose that's the right word. Years back, I should have been much quicker to latch on to human weaknesses and underline them, rather than be on the watch for how God gets His way through all lives, usually starting negatively, but ending up mighty positively. "Thinketh no evil." "Believeth all things." That's good! Of course the increasing recognition of some of my own weaknesses makes it much easier to overlook those of others!

I need not say more, as the memoirs tell their own tale. But for my fellow-workers in the Worldwide Evangelization Crusade and Christian Literature Crusade with whom Pauline and I have spent most of our lives, I should say, This is not an attempt at telling the story of the work and workers; I have done that in other books. It is merely an account of events and experiences and people both in and out of the Crusade with which and with whom we have been personally involved.

I hope man does not obtrude in these pages, but God in man and through man—on the eternal principle, "Out of weakness made strong."

NORMAN GRUBB

Fort Washington,
Pennsylvania, U.S.A.

I

Early Starts and Shocks

IT WOULD BE NO GOOD MY TRYING TO WRITE A MERELY FACTUAL autobiography. My life has been no more interesting or exceptional than thousands of others, and who would be bothered to read it except a few friends? Indeed, I could not look back and write disinterestedly, because of the change that took place at the age of eighteen, and the alteration that made in my life's aims and interests. It would be impossible for me to look even at my early years except in their relation to this central fact, whether contributing to it or detracting from it. So from this point of view I must write, and comment as I write.

I had the blessing of a good and happy home—except of course that there is no fundamental happiness to the youngest striving self when it can't attain what it really seeks. I was born on August 2, 1895. I had a wonderful father and mother. I had better mention their family backgrounds. But in doing so I hit the snag which still pops up above the surface in my old age—that ridiculous pride of class or culture or educational advantages. I suppose we English are particularly prone to it, but my loved American friends among whom I so enjoy living have it, too, in their own way! I am sure, and thankfully sure, that I have gained much through life from the type of folks my parents and relatives were, and the home and school upbringing I was given. It is obviously a case of having received much, much is required of me. But in the presence of God, the perfect Leveller, do our particular supposedly favoured backgrounds really mean that much?

If someone has had a tough upbringing, dragged up as we say, when God gets hold of him, are not his tough years a goldmine of experience with which to reach those I could never reach, and to do things with his own inherent gifts I could never do? I have surely learned that lesson among my fellow-workers in the missionary crusade to which I belong, as I have seen what God has done with so many of their lives with such different backgrounds from mine. So I see the foolishness of what I am still prone to, secret pride in family or education, or even present-day name-dropping of contacts with "important" people. "Cease ye from man whose breath is in his nostrils, for wherein is he to be accounted of?"

But still I am thankful for my early days. My father, Harry Percy Grubb, came of an old Irish family. I have somewhere the "family tree" one of the family members worked out, going back three hundred years. It traces us back to Ishmael Grubb of Ravensthorpe near Rugby, born in 1594. His son, John Grubb, born 1620, moved to Ireland in 1656. The pedigree claims that the family started with a certain Henricus von Grubbe in Denmark in 1040, and that the name originally means "a prince". My sister's comment is that she always thought it meant "a grave-digger"! My grandfather, with his family of eleven, owned the large house and grounds at Cahir, Co. Tipperary, called Cahir Abbey, and they were owners of the Corn Mills, the chief industry of the small town. But one of those family disasters happened over which families draw a veil. There was an unfortunate family speculation of nearly £100,000, a large sum for those days. The family had to sell the mill, and after his death the Abbey was sold. They had been members of the Society of Friends, and had earlier got into trouble with them, as the following document shows:

Whereas it has been the care of the Society of Friends or People called Quakers, to endeavour to guard its members from all amusements or entertainments of a hurtful or injurious tendency, and the practices of music and dancing, pursuits belonging to the vain and giddy world, being clearly of this class and utterly at variance with our principles, the Society has declared its entire disunity with them: and whereas Richard

Grubb Jnr, and Maria his wife who had their birthright and were educated in the said Society, have introduced and encouraged the practices of Music and Dancing in their house and have also attended those hurtful and injurious entertainments called Balls at which Music and Dancing form a chief part of the amusements, they have therefore been the objects of much concern to the body and have been repeatedly visited by appointment of this Meeting and much affectionate labour used to persuade them to relinquish these things and convince them of their hurtful tendency. But the care thus extended not having produced the desired effect, as they declined to discontinue the practice of Music nor would they agree to refrain from attending Balls, We therefore, feel it our duty to testify against their conduct and we do hereby disown the said Richard Grubb Jnr. and Maria his wife to be members of our religious Society; yet we desire that they may be favoured to see the inconsistency of these practices with the Christian character and that by submitting to the visitations of Divine Love they may be led into that life of self-denial and devotedness to their Creator which is acceptable in His sight.

Given forth by the Monthly meeting for the County of Tipperary held at Clonmel the 28th of 11th Month 1844 and in by order and on behalf thereof.

Signed by
William Davis (Clerk)

This is all I know of my grandparents, who died before my father married. Someone passed on to me a glass-framed replica of the Grubb Coat of Arms, described at the back for those who understand that language: Arms of the descendants of Samuel Grubb of Clonmel: Per chevron ermine and gules, en base a harp, or stringed argent, on a chief crenellee of the last three roses proper. Crest: a griphon's head erased per chevron crenellee sable and argent, charged with two roses in pale proper. Entered in the Register of the Office of Arms in Ireland. Volume J, Folio 141. G. O. Bentehaill, Athlone Pursuivant, Registrar of the Office. And beneath the Coat of Arms the words "Bonne et assez belle". We surely love to pat ourselves on the back!

My father was a gentle, humble, scholarly servant of the Lord Jesus Christ. Educated at the best college of Southern

Ireland, Trinity College, Dublin, he gained his M.A. and continued his studies in Switzerland by which he became so proficient in French and German that he could preach in either. He was a considerable Hebrew scholar. He also was a great lover of German literature and the German people. He constantly read German poetry. He was ordained into the Church of England, I believe with his parents' disapproval, saying he would surely starve. I do not know how God called him into the ministry, but he never looked back. He did not marry till forty-four, when he was already prematurely bald (a condition which has been obviously inherited by my two brothers, though not by me), and white, with a small neat beard. He was not a boys' man, and I am ashamed to think of how in my teen years I would really despise him and make fun of him; yet in all my years since as I look back, I have held him in deepest respect and love.

He and my mother sacrificed everything they could on their meagre parson's salary to give us four the happiest home and best education that we could have: and they gave us just that. His way of seeking to inculcate deeper things into my life was to take me for a walk nearly every day of the holidays, and talk as we walked, often about some Scripture upon which he was then meditating. Quite meaningless and a boredom I tried to escape, but it has left me with the lasting impression of a father who cared for us and was concerned for us. He was really a student and scholar more than preacher, but a true pastor to his people, first in the little village of Oxton near Nottingham; then in Macclesfield, a silk town near Manchester; and finally in Poole, near Bournemouth. And I can still see him as I would open his study door (because I knew he kept a box of chocolates in the desk) on his knees by the desk, his bald head upheld by one hand and sometimes asking me to come and join him in prayer.

My mother, Margaret Adelaide Crichton-Stuart, was a brilliant, lively, loving little lady, loving all and loved by all. Her background socially was different and had the so-called blue-blood touch in it. Her grandfather was Lord James Stuart, brother of the then Marquess of Bute. A former Marquess as Earl of Bute was deeply involved with the American Revolution, as Prime Minister in George the Third's time. So I have that much connection with my American cousins! The Bute family gradually acquired great wealth, owning Cardiff Castle and much of the Cardiff Docks, and Mount Stuart, the home on the Isle of Bute, from which they originally took their title, the family name being Crichton-Stuart. I have had no personal connections with the family, which I regret, nor did the wealth come this way! They joined the Roman Catholic Church in Queen Victoria's day. My mother's father, James Crichton-Stuart, was in the Foreign Office, but he died young and I never knew him.

He married a member of another brilliant family, Huguenot in origin, Fanny Adelaide Labouchere. All of England in Victorian days knew her brother, Henry Labouchere, as the notorious liberal—indeed radical—member of Parliament, commonly called Labby. He was scurrilous, left-wing, revolutionary, a thorn in the flesh of the Establishment and a *bête noire* to the Queen. He edited a paper called *Truth* which certainly did good in those times by exposing corruption of many kinds, and was the sworn enemy of the respectable London *Times*. Labby was, I am sorry to say, a mocker to his end in all matters of faith. It is said that when dying, a lamp caught fire by his bedside and he quipped even at that moment, "Flames? Not yet!" But he certainly had much of that French mercurial brilliance, and so had his sister, my grandmother. We loved her.

She lived in a big house in Bournemouth, which she sold to a Russian Princess and is now an hotel; and then another smaller house, Rockland St. Mary, but still quite big, where we were with her every summer. She was the real old Victorian aristocrat, in her long beautiful black dresses sweeping the ground, her white cap, her soft beringed hands, her lovely face. Her companion was always with her, Miss Nichols, who faithfully cared for her and read to her, though much, I fear, to my grandmother's contempt, for she wouldn't know whether Persia was in Europe or Asia, and whether this famous man was Conservative or Liberal (no Labour those days!). I don't know how my grandmother put up each summer for six weeks with us four little brats and our governess, but she did, and played games in the evenings with us. She really loved the Lord and was a loyal evangelical churchwoman, and was especially interested in the Lord's coming. I gathered she never really accepted Father, not thinking that an Irish clergyman was quite up to her daughter and I believe would never give him a son-in-law's kiss! But I, as a loyal Irishman, entirely differ with her on that!

Mother was thirteen years younger than Father, and from all I ever saw they had a wonderfully harmonious life. In our home they certainly lived as they preached. Mother, the opposite to Father, was thoroughly a young people's lover. She had a great Sunday Y.W.C.A. class for over three hundred young women in Boscombe before she married. She was much involved in London with the Christian activities for the "upper classes" that centred round the first Lord Radstock's home in Portman Square, where Mother also lived for a time. She could rattle off lists of names of Lord This and Lady That who were either our relatives or touched by the Radstock witness. This had reached right into the aristocracy surrounding the Tsar of Russia where there were many wonderful converts, and curiously I found later that my wife's uncle, Sir Kynaston Studd, had married one of them, the Princess Lieven.

But Mother was equally at home in the parish life, and a wholehearted fellow-worker with Father. That did not prevent her from being what I would think the ideal mother. She just seemed to be the loving servant of us children. "Mother this and Mother that", and Mother always there. She just made home for us. And with us four, she took the two children of close missionary friends, Mr. and Mrs. Lillingston Price, who were working among the Bhil Tribe in India; and for about ten years Gladys (later called Joan and

becoming Mrs. Warren Reeve) and Cecil Price were as much
of the family as we four.

My childhood years were in the vicarage of the little
country village of Oxton, near Robin Hood's Sherwood
Forest. In the normal way of a middle-class clergyman's
family of those days, there were always two servants, cook
and housemaid, and a governess. I am glad of that taste in
my young days of England's unmatchable countryside. It has
left something permanent in me—that little wood to which
Miss Turner, our favourite governess, and we used to walk
out and there be entranced in the springtime by the carpets of
primroses, bluebells and forget-me-nots, with the song of the
birds and the occasionally exciting glimpse of a pheasant or
even a fox. I still challenge the world to produce anything
equal to the English countryside in spring! There was a small
lake too, in the grounds of the Hall, the home of the Squire
of the village, Capt. Sherbrooke, R.N., and he allowed us
boys to go fishing perch, roach and eels.

I don't think anything further is worth mentioning of those
early years—golden years they seem now, like Wordsworth's
visions of youth which he always mourned the loss of; but in
fact they return in far more wonderful visions of beauty when
we begin all over again to see God's world with God's eyes!
There were the usual visits to watch the forge and the fire
blown up by the bellows, and the glowing iron on the anvil,
the clang of the heavy hammer and the horses being shod.
There was our favourite farmer, Mr. Bowstead, who, having
a round, shiny and wholly bald head, of course we called
"The Knob of Oxton". We appreciated watching the
chickens, pigs and cattle, and eating the box of chocolates he
always brought on Christmas Day.

SALUTARY SHOCKS AT PREP. SCHOOL

My conscious sorrows started when I was sent off to a boys'
preparatory school—South Lodge, Lowestoft, on England's
bleak east coast; about fifty boys; run by a good couple, the
Rev. W. R. Phillips and his wife, whom of course we called

"Dick and Ma Dick". They gave us a good educational background in the Classics, Latin, Greek, English literature and the rest. There was a quiet Christian tone, with daily prayers, Sunday church services, Mr. Phillips being a sincerely convinced Church of England clergyman. In later years, to my surprise, he got great light through the writings of "C.H.M.", the Plymouth Brethren expositor of the Scriptures, whose five famous little books on the Pentateuch have been living food for many, including myself. To "Dick", as a clergyman, they were like rich, hidden and suddenly discovered treasure.

Mr. Phillips' brother, Arthur, was an assistant master, who had lived long in Australia and fascinated us boys, claiming, quite apocryphally I now think, to have been a member of the Australian Test Team. We used to walk daily, two by two in a long file, to the playing fields, and our aim was to be one of the boys who could grab the chance of walking with "Mr. Arthur" at the end of the line and getting Australian stories out of him.

We played cricket, soccer and hockey (field hockey as Americans call it), the usual games in English boarding-schools. I reached the school team in all three, not very hard out of fifty boys, as wicket-keeper in cricket, and right half in both soccer and hockey.

That was the happier side of things. There was another side. For all the ten years I had in boarding-school, in this one and in the one I went on to, I hated school and never ceased to hate it. I hated returning after the holidays and counted the days to the end of the term, living only to get home. I don't know why, except that I terribly wanted to be popular but was not so, and knew nothing in those days of how to love others if you want to be loved!

I must just have been a nasty little boy at home, at least so I am now told—pinching the little girls sitting next to me in Sunday School, bossing my brothers and sisters around (I was number two of the six of us); and so without doubt a dose of boarding-school was just the right medicine for me. In my

18

cockiness I would follow the school hero around, Jarrold the fast bowler, and pull his coat tails, and I had one sure weapon: if he hit or pushed me around, I would scream at the top of my voice. I had yet to learn that to "sneak" on another fellow, or to cry or scream when hurt is the unforgivable sin of an English schoolboy.

At last some of the boys had had enough of it and carried me down to the basement and dumped me in the coal hole. But my piercing screams reached the ears of Mr. Phillips. Severe punishment (I had it twice) was when the terrible words were spoken by him, "Go up to the Bow Room." This was a large bow-windowed dormitory room. Here the victim had to remove his trousers and the cane was applied with real force on the bare flesh, while the school stood silent in the corridor below to catch the sounds of the strokes or the moans of the sufferer. And then the victim would come down, descend to the basement and there in the lavatory display his weals to a few chosen admirers. But on this occasion Mr. Phillips laid hold of a boy named Bird who had taken the lead in consigning me to the coal hole, and off he was taken to the Bow Room. I then was shown by him on his return what the cane did to him, and it had done plenty, real red weals across him. Not only did this really shake me, but Mr. Phillips himself then took me aside and said he never wished to hear a boy screaming like that to get other boys into trouble, and next time it would be me for the Bow Room. That finished it for me and I learned one valuable lesson for life. Never again would a person get a peep from me, and they didn't.

Perhaps that is one of the good effects of the boarding-school system on the English character—courage, endurance, take your medicine without whining, admit your faults but never sneak on the other fellow! I needed putting in my place and I surely got it! Perhaps the bad effects are the reserve of us English; we hide our feelings, run miles from expressing emotion; and I believe that is a real hindrance to many of our English public-school type, preventing us from admitting our need of God and from coming out from under the cover of a formal Anglican Faith to an embarrassing enthusiasm for Jesus Christ!

There were other dark spots. I came from a generation where the functions of the body were not discussed and nothing was said on sex. So I picked up from a casual remark of another boy the misuse of my body; and this became my secret bugbear, guilt and failure, until I was eighteen. No one said a thing to me nor I to anybody, I would have been far too ashamed, and yet that incessant guilt and failure became, as the Bible says, the operation of God's law on me which brings the knowledge of sin, and in the end brought me to the ultimate point of accepting Christ. So thank God for the redemptive use of our sins!

I ended my five years at South Lodge top of the school for two years, but in one of them with equal marks with my life-long friend, later Dr. Murray Webb-Peploe of the Dohnavur Fellowship of India; and this was a shame for me as Murray is a year younger than I, but that much more brilliant! I am thankful for South Lodge. The dark spots were either of my own making, or are the usual type of sex battles that all have to face one way or another till we find the true meaning and purpose of our marvellous human make-up; and without doubt the same kind of thing takes place in all schools. But it was a good educational start in life and I am grateful to my parents for affording it for me. One other good memory was the practice of the whole school memorizing a verse of Scripture every day, and on the last day of term, the whole fifty of us standing in a great circle in the gym and repeating the chapter by memory, verse by verse, as each took his turn. I can proudly say that for several years I got 100 per cent at that event, and it did plant some chapters unforgettably in my memory, such as John 14, Romans 8 and 1 Corinthians 15.

To my own surprise and delight and that of my parents, the school put me in for the scholarship examination for one of our greatest public schools, Marlborough College, where fifteen annual scholarships are offered for sons of clergymen; and I came out third that year. If it had not been for that, my parents could not have sent me to such a first-class school. I also added to that a second scholarship more difficult to get, the year after, which meant that two-thirds of the cost were met.

LIFE IN AN ENGLISH PUBLIC SCHOOL—MARLBOROUGH COLLEGE

At thirteen, the usual age for an English public school, in the year 1909, I started in Marlborough. (My American friends will understand that what we call a public they call a private school—boarding and for boys only.) I appreciate now what I didn't then, my great privilege this next five years in being in one of our great public schools. That it was right at the top in its educational standards was best judged in my day by the number and level of scholarships gained at Oxford and Cambridge. The school had six hundred boys, divided into a number of houses of about fifty each. All the boys were boarders. So there we were, herded together yearly for three terms of about three months each.

Marlborough College is situated on the Wiltshire Downs, bracing and healthy, though definitely cold in years long before central heating; isolated also, as it is surrounded by miles of Downs on one side and the Savernake Forest on the other. It is on the edge of the small town of Marlborough with then about two thousand inhabitants, the town being out of bounds for most of the school most of the time. All the boys wore the same black coats with striped trousers, collar and black tie, with a school cap. The top athletes of the school, the "bloods" in the school teams, were distinguished by special ties and caps.

All boys had the school custom of carrying "kishes", a kind of padded cushion an inch or two thick which folded in two, and the books were carried in it under the arm. The idea of the kish originated to make sitting easier on the hard school benches. The inside of the cushion was of various colours, but the school team members had "blood kishes" with special house colours in them. They alone were also privileged to wear grey flannel trousers, called "grey barnes". Conditions certainly were severe, and the food definitely poor (much improved of late, I hear). A famous stodgy pudding, ill-tasting, called "College Bolly", was served as second course at lunch several days a week. I think it was certainly an economy to the college, as we would eat as little as possible of it, partly because of its nastiness and partly as being no good preparation for an afternoon on the football field!

As in South Lodge, I was definitely unhappy at Marlborough. I think the main reason was unsatisfied ambition. My studies never interested me. It is a wonder I came through as well as I did. I just went through them mechanically and with no living interest. Indeed, I did not really awake mentally until my thirties, and since then I have been an avid student. My passion was the school games. I dreamed of the possibility of getting into the rugger, cricket or hockey teams. The team members, the "bloods", were my idols. I have never, until quite recent years, got over the secret longing and inner fantasies of being a great rugger or cricket player. I would imagine myself running through for a try, or scoring a dramatic century, to the roars of a football crowd or the modest clapping of the cricket spectators. I suppose that is why the sporting pages of the papers have always had my attention. In point of fact, I never reached near eminence in any of them. The nearest I have ever come is marrying a daughter of one of England's greatest cricketers! And how little he ever talked of it!

Combined with the passionate ambition to be a great games player was my intense desire to be popular, and if possible with some of these "bloods". That has had, I think, a permanent effect on me in giving me an almost undue respect for those superior to me, and I suppose an underlying inferiority complex. I am not quickly at ease in their presence.

In those Marlborough years I first found out what it is to be really unpopular! Marlborough has a junior house, called A House, into which you enter before going on to the senior house of your choice. By my fourth and last term in A House, I was captain of my dormitory of about fifteen. To keep order, I had power to make boys bend over and beat with the gym shoe, but not with the cane. Only prefects and masters could use that. I don't know why I obviously annoyed my dormitory, and even my assistant captain, Jerome by name. But one evening he incited them to make trouble, so I lined them up in turn and beat them, including Jerome himself.

There is also a strange custom by which senior boys can say "Turf" to a junior, and he has to get out of your way or give you his seat. Next morning early, Sunday morning, I awoke to find my captain's bed in the corner surrounded by Jerome and the boys with threatening looks. So I immediately said, "Turf." But no good. I was reminded that that law had no effect before 8 a.m. So then they solemnly dragged me from my bed and inflicted the last of humiliations on me. The centre of the long room with beds up both sides was occupied by a long washtable with a series of holes to hold fifteen basins (washing in cold water, of course). At the middle of the table was a gap of several feet, a kind of cage, in which were stored all the pots during the day, which the maid put under each bed for the night, and the cage stood empty. Into it they shoved me and shut the cage. And there I was, the dormitory captain, until the hour came when I could legitimately use my powers and demand my release.

I shall never forget my sense of wounded humiliation as I sat at breakfast that morning, knowing all the house was agog with the news! I don't remember more, though I think I have carried a sensitiveness through life from that incident. But I am sure it also did me a power of good and deflated a whole balloonful of inordinate conceit!

My five years at Marlborough passed without much incident. As a scholarship boy I started not in the lower forms but halfway up the school, in the form called "Shell". And from there gradually through the Lower and Upper Fifth, to

the Lower Sixth and finally to the Upper Sixth, which consisted of about the twenty top boys of the school. I was in the
Upper Sixth for my last year, and a school prefect, which entitled me to the privilege of wearing a white tie on Sundays,
and to use the cane for disciplinary purposes in my house.
But as I say, my work was never my heart's interest, and I
couldn't have given much inspiration to my masters—
"beaks" as we called them.

Marlborough being founded with a special interest in the
sons of the clergy, we had services in the very fine school
chapel every morning and evening. I can't think it did me
much good. I remember nothing. The Church of England
service was regularly read, which may have conditioned my
life's repulsion for prayers and services by rote. I can't
remember the gist of any Sunday sermon, except just one
small yet important touch. There were two masters named
Hewett, two brothers, and we called them "Old Dog" and
"Young Dog". I have heard since that Old Dog had a real
experience of Christ; I don't know, but I do remember that
once when he was preaching, something must have been said
which caused me to say, "Accept salvation through Jesus as
a gift? No, it can't be as easy as that." But it was obviously
a seed sown.

My only moment of minor glory was in Rugby football—
rugger as we called it. I had no real talent or training in it;
we had no systems of training for our school games that came
within miles of the way I now find to be the normal practice
in American schools. But, maybe because of my Irish blood,
I could make wild and fearless dashes into things. My house,
C3, had a very poor reputation for games, quite at the bottom;
but in my fourth year we had a great house captain, Philip
Margetson, destined later to become Sir Philip Margetson,
Commissioner of the London Police. He really put some fire,
spunk and daring into us. We were in the minor league
division, but managed somehow to get to the top of it.

This gave us a right to challenge the head of the major
division to a cockhouse match. The thing was an absurdity,

for they, Sandford's, were far and away the strongest in the school. I guess the school turned out to watch a farce. But Margetson had put some guts into us. They had a star outside three-quarter, the fastest runner in the school team, Procter. I am sure he thought he would just run rings round us whenever he pleased. I was full-back for our team, and one job of the full-back is to "collar" the fellow with the ball by going low for him below where he could "hand you off", and fling yourself against him at about knee height. And this I did with my Irish verve and abandon. I suppose Procter had not thought I was worth trying to swerve around, so down he came again and again with the ball to the cheers of the boys on the touch-line, for the English are always on the side of the weaker.

A full-back also has the job of falling on the ball when the eight forwards make a concerted rush, dribbling the ball with their feet to break right through for a touch-down. To fall on the ball meant throwing yourself to the ground at the feet of the rushing eight, with your back to them, and as you do that, grabbing the ball and holding on to it. This effectively breaks the rush and there has to be a "scrum". This also was the daring type of thing that suited me, and down I went and frustrated them again and again. The amazing result was that poor little C3 was actually leading for half the game, and Sandford's only won in the end by a margin. I didn't know that I was the school hero for a few days!

I was then given a trial in a "Big Game" for the School XV (a rugby side has fifteen members). I was hurt in that game, but while I was in the "San" recovering, the time came for the house captains to vote in the new members of the LX (the school third team. I don't know why the first team is the XV, the correct number of players; but the second is called the XL, and the third the LX). When the clapping was over, as the names were announced, I was top of the list for the LX; and a week later, more voting, more announcements, more clapping and I was voted in top of the XL. That gave me the coveted privilege of a handsome cap of dark blue velvet fringed with silver, and a beautiful tassel of a bundle of thick silk threads. I still have it! I had become a minor blood!

And that was the limit of my glory! But God knows his business. The last year came round, and with the previous year's reputation I had serious hopes of making the School XV as full-back; and I was house captain. But at the very first "Big Game"—trial game, while I had my leg in the air, punting, I was collared by a powerful master named Stagg, who was also playing, and down I went with my leg twisted under me—a torn cartilage, and out for the season. So far as my real football value was concerned, I think it was a merciful release from a big disappointment, because I don't think I had what it took for the school full-back, and the man who got it, Blech, was the better. But it meant something far more important to me, though I did not see it as such then.

As I lay in the hospital after the operation, just one thought suddenly crossed my mind, Is life wholly selfish? It seemed to be a sudden eye-opener to me of my own self-centredness. Everything was for me. My mother was for me, and my father was for me, the whole world was for me. Was there no better meaning to life than that? It was one of those inner words from the Spirit.

I returned to school for my last two terms. My football ambitions were destroyed, but I still had that intense desire to be the friend and intimate of the leaders in the school. One especially was Sidney Woodroffe, who in a couple of years would be dead on the battlefield of France, but whose bravery was immortalized by the posthumous award of the Victoria Cross, England's highest award, equivalent to the Medal of Honor in the U.S.A. I would give anything to have a word from him, to be allowed, as happened once or twice, to visit him in his study, and I suffered through jealousy of another boy who became his obvious favourite. So I was still never happy, never reaching my goals.

How proud I was when he invited me, with about twenty others, to have a photo taken before we left, with him sitting in the centre. I still have that picture. The majority of those splendid fellows laid down their lives on the battlefields.

Boys' schools obviously have their moral problems. One is the "tart" system, by which older boys single out pretty-looking young boys for immoral purposes. How wonderfully God kept His hand on me. I suppose I was one of those pretty boys. When I was still in the Junior House, one fellow in the School XV, therefore a demi-god to me when just a new boy, somehow got in touch with me and asked me to go walking with him out on the Downs. We went several times. Macarthur was his name. I was innocent and had no idea what the aims of such walks would be. Yet he never said one word or did one thing out of place. We just walked and talked. What reason would a big boy, a school "blood", have for risking himself (because surely he would have been in trouble if discovered) for just some walks and harmless talks with a little kid? I would say God's protective power. There was another older boy, this time one of the most brilliant batsmen in the cricket team, who I could see in chapel had his eye on me. I still did not know what all this led to, but somehow I recoiled from wanting any acquaintance with him.

I am sure the quiet moral influence of my good and happy home had its restraining effect on me. There were boys who loved to tell dirty stories and talk of sex, and I loved to listen to them, and enjoyed it. But somehow I could never participate in that kind of talk, beyond silent enjoyment. And the same with swearing. There were the boys, just the one or two, who would tell us of the sex relations they had with girls in the holidays or claimed that they could slip away at night when at school (I rather doubt that). But certainly that kind of thing was not rampant, at least out in the open, as it appears to be in schools today. I personally still think that separate boys' and girls' schools at that age are better, and the risk and practice of some homosexuality less harmful than the open sex relations in co-educational schools.

MY SPIRITUAL WATERLOO

Those Easter holidays were my spiritual Waterloo. I had begun to question the reality of God and Christ. I was reading such books as John Stuart Mill's *Utilitarianism*. I had not lost my boyhood faith nor jettisoned it. But I was questioning. If I was selfish, was not God also? Did it not say, "For Thy pleasure we are and were created"? and of Jesus that "For the joy set before Him, He endured the cross"? What difference between their self-interest and mine? Yet at the same time as I had my youthful intellectual questioning, I was battling with and had the guilt of my secret moral defeats.

There was a friend in Bournemouth—my father had by now moved to a church in Poole, near Bournemouth—who was a retired Royal Artillery major, an original, interesting fellow, named Major Gartside-Tippinge. He had a lovely home and grass tennis-court. He was also a very keen Christian and especially keen on getting boys to Christ. His wife was a sister of D. E. Hoste, the General Director of the China Inland Mission. He used to invite my brother Harold and me over to tennis, and then, if he could, catch us after in his drawing-room for a talk about our need of salvation, which we called having a "pi-jaw". On one such visit, my brother escaped somehow, but I was caught in the drawing-room. All I remember Tippinge asking me was the pertinent question, Did I belong to Christ?

He had caught me, or rather the Spirit of God through him. If he had asked did I belong to the church of which I was a member, that would have been easy. Wasn't I the son of a parson, baptized and confirmed in the Church of England? But when he asked me if I had a personal relationship to Christ, I was caught. How could I say I had a personal relationship with a Person whose existence I was doubting? I was embarrassed. With my public school code of hiding our feelings on such subjects as religion, I could lie my way out, say I did, and escape. I did not realize then that our eternal

28

destiny hangs on our honesty; and as Jesus said, in John 3, when light comes to us we either hate it or respond to it, and are either saved or lost accordingly. Somehow I did manage to admit that I could not say He was personal to me. Tippinge got me on my knees, made me pray something, and I got up as I got down, and escaped.

But on my way home on the top of a tramcar, the implication of what I had said got its teeth into me. I knew the gospel, and that, if I could not say Christ was my personal Saviour, I was going to hell. And I knew too, through the guilt of my sins, that I deserved to go there. At last this was real to me; so as soon as I reached my small bedroom at the top of the house, I got on my knees and for the first time in my life meant it when I asked, according to the Lord's prayer, for my sins to be forgiven.

Immediately there flashed into my mind what I had always been taught but it had meant nothing to me—that that was why Jesus died—to take away my sins. Then, with a strange new sense of joy and relief, I said, "If that is so, I don't have to go to hell, God is my Father, and heaven is my home." In succeeding years I may have dug deeper in order to understand in a more complete sense—at least for my own satisfaction—what those simply stated and believed facts really mean; but these were the simple gospel facts by which I, and millions of others, have "passed from death unto life", and "the Spirit had borne witness with my spirit" that I was a child of God.

The next thought that came into my mind, true again to our school traditions of downgrading emotion, was that this was just a momentary emotion, and tomorrow morning I would wake up thinking football, not Christ. But not so. My first waking thoughts were this new joy, and have been so now these fifty-four years! And two facts stand out to me—first, I am glad there are bold men who go out of their way to seek you out and ask if you are Christ's; and secondly, that I had had the background years of church and Bible teaching, boring though it was to me, because it had stored my mind with the truths of the way of salvation, ready material for my heart's need when the moment came. And though this crisis moment stands out to me, and I suppose will do throughout eternity, I really know that it was the background life and love and example of my parents which had prepared the soil and sown the seed, so that I had never been without a sincere faith (even if temporarily shaken), said my prayers, read my Bible, and had moral restraints on me. So April 1914 was the turning-point of my life, and I was eighteen years of age.

I did not realize, as I do now, what had really happened to me, and what happens every time a person gets born from above. My hungry, ambitious, dissatisfied self had found a new centre—not itself. A love for Christ, and for the Father who had sent Him, had begun to supersede love for just myself. It was not really my love for Him, for I am only capable of self-love; it was, as Paul said, "the love of God" (not my love for God, but His own love) "shed abroad in our hearts by the Holy Spirit who is given to us" (Rom. 5:5). In other words, an inner unity had taken place, my human spirit with His Spirit, branch to Vine as Jesus said. I had "come home". I had been one who had lost his way and had lived in the illusion (but real enough to us while we believe it, for we are what we believe) of being a separate little human seeking my own ends and fighting my own, usually losing, battles of life.

By coming home, like the prodigal to the father, I had found my restoration to the One Spirit of the universe, the Eternal Father through His Son; and that restoration is a union, spirit with Spirit (1 Cor. 6:17), by which I am an expression of Him in my human form; and despite my multiple deviations in my free and temptable humanity, the new spontaneous motivation of my human self is loving Him more than I love myself; and in loving Him, loving all. My self-love, instead now of finding its expression in seeking my own self-ends, begins to find a new meaning in pleasing myself by pleasing Him and wanting others to know Him. In place of being basically a self-lover, I had begun to be a God- and

y Father and Mother, the
v. H. P. and Mrs. Grubb

Their four children,
1910

l. to r.: Norman,
Harold, Violet,
Kenneth

Norman Grubb in the Gloucester Regiment (1914–19)

other-lover; or should I say, I had begun to be the kind of self-lover God Himself is, who loves Himself by loving His creation. His self-pleasing is His self-giving.

The first simple form that it took for me was a letter to my mother saying that Christ had become a personal Saviour to me—in other words, I now began to honour Christ more than magnify myself. The second was when I returned for my last term to Marlborough. I knew nothing about a "duty to witness" or any such legalistic imposition on my fresh experience; but at least to one intimate friend, Henry de Candole, head of the house (and later Bishop of Knaresborough), I confided what had happened. His comment was, "Well, if that is real Christianity, none of us have it!" (though I am glad that has not remained true of Henry through the years!).

CHRIST ALL OR NOT AT ALL

And now came the day that changed the history of our world: August 4, 1914. The Kaiser's Germany invaded Belgium. Britain, true to her pledge to Belgium, declared war on Germany. An immense enthusiasm swept through Britain. There was only one possible response for a young man—Get to the front line. Get to the trenches. I lived for this. Could any young man be a young man and not want to take his place in the front line? Maybe it was my Irish temperament taking over again!

I had been in the O.T.C. (Officers' Training Corps) in Marlborough, and had passed Certificate A, which meant that I was supposedly fitted to be an officer in a Citizen Volunteer Army, and I wore a red badge on the sleeve of my military tunic to indicate this. I had sat for the scholarship examinations for Oxford and Cambridge, and I had been awarded an Exhibition to one of the smaller Cambridge colleges, Sidney Sussex (Oliver Cromwell's college). An Exhibition is a kind of consolation prize for those not up to full scholarship standard (and one must add that those scholarships are of the very top level), yet who had some intellectual standing, and were not just duds. But of course now, instead of Cambridge, it was the army. In September I received my call-up and commission as a second lieutenant of the 9th Battalion of the Gloucester Regiment. A thrilling moment.

At this close of my public school days, I can only say that I can never be thankful enough for the privilege of being in a school like Marlborough. Of course I had, and have described, some of my boyhood battles. All must have them; but the educational standards and the character building of Marlborough are such that I congratulate any boy who gains entry there, and any parents who can send their sons there.

Another crisis, of far more importance than my commission, was to intervene before I joined my battalion. I had, of course, reached the stage when I was interested in girls. I don't know why, because of my upbringing I suppose, I have always had a great respect for the other sex, lasting right up to today, and a marvel that they would have anything to do with rough and crude creatures like ourselves; and I think that has gone a long way in preserving me, by God's mercy, from seeking to take false advantage of women. Indeed, the first sudden affection for a woman of about forty, the daughter of one of the leading families near us, of which she never knew a thing, brought me up sharp to a new attitude and control over my own body, which was a great relief and release.

But the first deep affection I had was for a beautiful girl, daughter of near neighbours, a coal-merchant and mayor of the town, about four years older than I. We really did love each other in a boy–girl fashion, and we had many nights' walks in the park together, and constant correspondence, and she was the first girl I ever daringly kissed! But beyond that, the kind of relationship which seems so tragically and wickedly common today between the unmarried was never even in my thoughts. We loved and hugged as boy and girl, and that was all. But she had certainly captured my heart, though with no thought of marriage. Young Englishmen didn't think of marriage in their teens! But then I told her of how Christ had become my personal Saviour. She could not see this. Good church girl—but not this. We carried on until about three weeks before I was due to join my battalion.

A favourite uncle, the Rev. George C. Grubb, who had a great spiritual influence on my life, and whom I loved greatly, full of Irish fun yet filled with the love of God, was staying with us. He was world-famous in evangelical and Keswick Convention circles for his great missions, especially in Australia. It was the great number brought to Christ in the Church of England in New South Wales that gave the Sydney diocese and the Archbishopric its evangelical foundations which have lasted till today. The story of those missions, and others among planters in Ceylon and elsewhere, were recorded in a much read book at that time, *What God hath wrought*, and a second one, *The Same Lord*, and a series of his living talks in *Unsearchable Riches*. He was also one of the constant platform speakers in the early Keswick Conventions.

This Uncle George gave me a little booklet. I don't remember its contents except that it was like handing me a red-hot poker. It was suddenly burned into me that I could not have both Christ and one who was against Christ in the centre of my heart. How I fought this and remember throwing the booklet on the floor and wishing I had never seen it. This was a far fiercer battle than anything involved in accepting Christ. Why should I not keep both the girl and Christ? Our relationship was a healthy friendship. But the Voice persisted. You cannot have both. If you hold to her, you lose Christ. It was like a hell, and I was travelling to and fro to Salisbury ordering and buying my subaltern's uniform. What agonizing journeys those were. I tried my father. He was permissive and left me with the impression that I could keep both. But that Voice persisted. Finally, I tried my mother, and that was the end of it. She made me see that a real choice was involved. So I made it. We live where we love, and when the chips were down, Christ was my love.

I now see what was truly involved in this. Sins are dealt

with when we come to Christ, at least as far as deliberately living in sin is concerned. Idols are not sin, but right things in wrong places. The human heart can only have one supreme affection at its centre. An idol is a rival affection, and, while the rival occupies the affections, our interests and activities go along with it. I loved Christ, but my daily interests were around the girl. When at last, on one of those train journeys, I made the decision and dropped the girl, a sudden new thought took possession of me. I was soon going to be with a crowd of men and any of us might be dead in a year. I had found the gift of eternal life. I had better see that some of them find it.

When previously I had only spoken of Christ in a casual comment to a friend, it now was a life's obsession. I had really found my life's calling, and life's meaning for me—that others should find the Christ I had. But I could not see this, it could not dawn on me, while my affections and interests were in another direction. Christ must be Lord as well as Saviour. A Rubicon was crossed, really the second stage of the new birth. I fear it must have hurt the girl and without the meaning it had for me, except the realization from her point of view that I had become a fanatic; but of course it had to end sometime as we were not contemplating marriage, and she has now long since been married.

FIVE YEARS AS SOLDIER AND WITNESS

I enjoyed my army years, five of them. It was the life that suited me, and near the end I considered taking a permanent commission, which was possible in war days for volunteer officers without going through Sandhurst.

Because of my recent experience, the army life, my duties as a soldier and the outcome of the war were not my major interest, nor were having fun with my fellow-officers in the Mess or indulging myself. We had a year's training at home, and we surely needed it. What must a callow youth straight from school, with no experience of the world and mighty little of soldiering, have seemed like to the forty men in my

34

charge as my platoon, men from between eighteen and maybe thirty-five, who had been wage-earners in the world, probably from sixteen years old onwards? They must have had some laughs behind my back! But my interest was in speaking to all about Christ, and it cost me everything to do it.

I hated broaching the subject, and it had to be like repeated jumps off the deep end. One of my first and crudest attempts was on a wet and muddy day when we were under canvas. I heard the clink of coins in a tent as I passed. I knew that meant gambling, which was against army regulations. So gathering up my courage, I opened the fly of the tent, popped my head in and said, "I say, you men, I can tell you something better than gambling, and that is to have Jesus Christ." And on I went! I would talk to the sergeant marching beside me on our route marches, or to my fellow-officer, even my company commander *en route* to a parade, and that cost something. And many of those I spoke to were dead a year later. The first man I ever helped to accept Christ was a fellow-subaltern named Hone. It had cost me when lying outside our tents on a Sunday afternoon, to open my Testament and read. He saw me, made some interested comment and accepted Christ. I don't think he went on particularly well; he is a barrister today.

My witness was a mixed one. I was entirely ignorant of what a Christian should or should not do to set an example. I had dropped the little smoking I did before I was converted, and did not drink. But my chief friend in the battalion was Roger Fowke, a slightly older man who was a captain and company commander. He also was a keen Christian but of a broader outlook than mine, and a great follower of Donald Hankey whose book, *A Student in Arms*, was in vogue then.

As I talked with Roger, he advised me to be as much in the world with the fellows as one could, and thus make one's witness more acceptable to them. So I took up smoking and continued it all through the war, especially enjoying my pipe, which indeed I could still enjoy! And my taste in cigarettes was always for "Turks" more than "Gaspers"! Also drinking in the Mess. Fortunately I never took to spirits and couldn't stand whisky the few times I drank it; but I drank beer, and shandy, the popular mixture of beer and ginger-beer. I would also go to dances, though not able to dance, but at least I could sit out with the girls and talk to them about the Lord! I would take packets of cigarettes around with me to the men's rooms when we were billeted for the winter in Cheltenham, and then talk to them of Christ. I founded a little Christian society under the initials of C.O., which in our case meant not Commanding Officer but Christ's Own. Quite a number joined, and we had as many as thirty young officers to a meeting. My own batman, Roberts, who continued with me for much of the war, had, I believe, truly given himself to Christ.

At last came the time for our embarkation for France and the front, the longed-for event! A few days before I got F. W. Dwelly, who was a live Church of England curate in Cheltenham, to come down for a last talk with the men of the battalion. Though probably broader in doctrine than I (though I did not know anything of these things in those days), he had a real living experience of Christ and we had become close friends. About four hundred crowded into a marquee, and very many signed the decision cards Dwelly handed out. Dwelly later became Dean of Liverpool and was largely responsible for the building of the new Anglican Cathedral.

I by no means think my witness was effective, either with officers or men. I knew so little myself; but I can say it was my one consuming objective. For this reason I never found the normal attractions of the world a pull. Smoking, drinking, dancing, movies, did not really interest or hold me, except as a means of witness. I continued to have friendships with some very nice girls, one in particular, the daughter of a retired colonel in Cheltenham; but always with them, as elsewhere, to talk of Christ was my main interest. I did have fun with the fellows in the Mess, and one or two quite scary escapades, and was on good terms with my crowd of younger

36

officers, but they surely all knew what the conversation would be when we got to close quarters.

We were only three months in France, enough time to get our baptism of fire and front-line life in the trenches, which I found fascinating—the deep trench system, maybe 12 feet deep, sometimes the whole side of a trench built up with tins of bully beef out of the abundance of unused food supplies; deep dug-outs with wire beds when off duty: the fire-step, by standing on which you could peer over the top through our barbed-wire defences and see the Germans only a quarter mile away; the armies of rats, sometimes so thick that as one walked in the trenches one could not help stepping on one; our revolver practice in the evenings, shooting at them as they ran past in silhouette on the trench edge above us. Of course, they had ample food in the dead bodies in no-man's-land. Otherwise, it was a pretty quiet section of the line. And there one night I passed a fellow-officer, to discover it was my school-friend Mayo McClenagahan, with whom I had shared a study in Marlborough! Both he and his brother, such lovely fellows, were killed before the end. Why were such killed, and I spared?

Then we had sudden secret orders to move—down through the south of France, crowded on to a British battleship; and so to the new front being opened at Salonika, against the Bulgarians, allies of Germany—Salonika, the Thessalonica of Paul. But I am sorry now I wasn't sufficiently alive to the historical aspects of my Bible to make investigations. We were sent to a range of hills about 20 miles north of the city. There on the far side of the range we were set to work digging a defence system of trenches looking over to the quiet Lake Langaza in the plain below. On beyond was the farther range of mountains from which we expected attack by the Bulgars. They never came, so we dug away, hard work, as much was rock. In fact, a slab of rock was my bed for many months, good training for a pioneer missionary! The hills were a dream of beauty in the spring, clothed in anemones of every colour, and the home of dozens of tortoises, babies to big ones. Some fellows tried sending small ones home as pets in parcels!

During these Salonika months, I had a sharp lesson to learn. My Commanding Officer, Colonel Fane, was not one who approved my kind of Christian witness. He knew about it, and I had a regular little meeting going with a few of the men. He trumped up some charge to get my friend Roger Fowke, who was then a major in command of a company, sent home, but he failed in that. However, he did nicely catch me out. We had battalion inspection, and it certainly was true that I was not the smart officer with a smart platoon which I could have been if I had put the same heart into my military duties as into my Christian witness. After the inspection, he sent for me to tell me that mine was the most slovenly platoon in the battalion, and unless I improved, and that quickly, he would have me sent home in disgrace. That did hit me, and was just the medicine I needed.

I had slipped up in not realizing that Christian witness consists in being the best possible in the job assigned to one, as well as in speaking of Christ to others. I really got the point, and once again my Irish blood was aroused and I set to work to be the best. I did succeed, and, for instance, when I was sent for a bombing course (in the use of hand grenades by the infantry which were just then being developed), I came out top with recommendation for being promoted to Brigade Bombing Officer. But I think the colonel had a jaundiced eye on me by then, and I was never even promoted to first lieutenant, but was passed over. Through the whole war I never went beyond the "two pips" of a first lieutenant, while nearly all my early contemporaries became captains or majors. But I think I can claim that to some extent it was "for the gospel's sake", although I also learned a healthy lesson which has stood me well for life.

Often we officers in our idle hours would sit in a tent talking and smoking, and one I got close to was Stanley Stone, later adjutant of the battalion and mentioned in dispatches. Years after, back home one Sunday afternoon, I passed a familiar figure in a park near home. It was Stanley, and I found that by the severe illness and death of his loved elder son who had become a keen Christian, both Stanley and his wife, Gladys, had come to a living relationship with Christ, and our friendship has remained close ever since.

The end to my nine months in Salonika came suddenly. In a wind storm my tent was blown down. In extricating myself, my old football knee was twisted and dislocated again. I went by hospital ship to Valletta, Malta, to a very pleasant hospital there. My knee was further operated on, supposedly by an expert, but I doubt it. I had much pain and came out of it with an enlarged knee prone at all times to sinovitis. (I was later awarded a small government pension. However, as it did not prevent me from many good years of the use of it, trekking the jungles of Africa and elsewhere, I thought it only honourable to renounce the pension; and though I am now told it is full of arthritis, it still gives me little trouble except that I can't walk long distances, and long ago had to give up outdoor games.)

From Malta, after convalescence, I was drafted to another battalion of the Gloucester Regiment, the first fifth, in France. Here for a year I had experience of real war. My one moment of military glory came when the Germans were pulling back in 1917 from some territory, doubtless regrouping for their final big assault in 1918. We were detailed to follow them up in their retreat.

My company had to carry out a night attack and capture a certain Tombois Farm. My platoon was in reserve, about a mile behind, and we were lodged in what were obviously pigsties, but quite clean. While crouching quietly there, we received sudden information that the rest of the company had been caught on barbed wire and decimated. Orders were for us to proceed by ourselves and take the farm.

So I did what seemed the only possible thing, divided my platoon into halves, one half proceeding up one side of the road towards the farm, and the other on the other. A few shells fell, that was all. But what a stroke of what we call luck! When we neared the farm we found that the Germans had not extended their barbed wire over the road, but only cut down a tree or two across it. Over we got, and there we were behind their trench line and at the opening of a sunken road at right angles to the main road, common around French farms. There was only one thing to do, advance up this sunken road, taking the risk of finding ourselves among a hive of Germans.

It turned out that they had made dug-outs for themselves in the steep bank on the side of the sunken road facing towards us, and out from that bank on top had cut their defensive trenches, from which doubtless they had shot down our company. But they didn't know we had got behind them. As I slushed along in the mud of that road in the pitch darkness, with my sergeant and the platoon in single file behind, I heard two men approaching talking in loud German. Evidently they had no idea we were there. When near enough, I fired in the darkness. There was a splash or two and silence. We saw two bodies lying there in the morning. I don't know if these were the two because there were others in the vicinity. We then continued.

Whether the firing scared the Germans I don't know, but we found a series of empty dug-outs, some with lights still in them, and from one I tooked a curved German pipe as a souvenir. At the door of each dug-out, the only thing to do seemed to be to push it open with my shoulder, with a torch in one hand and revolver in the other, and take the chances. In only one was there a German, a little fellow, on his knees. The body of an officer or sergeant-major was stretched beside him, and I should think he was his batman. He was vociferously crying out "Kamerad, Kamerad" with his hands up. These were tense moments, because I was trying to shut him up for fear he would be warning the others by his cries, and put my revolver to his head with my finger on the trigger. The fellows behind kept saying, "Shoot him, sir, shoot him." I felt like doing it, but am glad I didn't. He looked pitiful on his knees, but in moments of tension one can do all sorts of things. However, I passed him back down the line of men as a prisoner.

As we went on, we saw Germans in front of us running across the sunken road and up the other side, and threw grenades at them. They did not fire on us. By morning light we found the farm was ours. That was all. Not very heroic, but it was reported to the authorities, and later came the announcement that I was given the Military Cross, and my sergeant the Military Medal. The Military Cross is a decoration for meritorious action for officers or warrant officers, a silver cross with a medal ribbon of a central band of purple and the two outside bands of white.

I had the kind of narrow shaves most of us had, and which made most of us say, Why did I escape and not the other fellow? Twice I had what came to me as a direct hunch or guidance, and it was good I obeyed it.

We were occupying an isolated forward trench in full sight of the Germans, about 1,000 yards away. From this trench a small communication trench led to an observation post 100 yards in advance. I was occupying this post with signallers and orderlies. In the morning the Germans laid a barrage on our main trench, but not on the forward post. Suddenly a clear word came to me, "Get out of your post and go back to where they are being shelled." I said to the others, "I'm going back to the trench. You fellows do what you like." I broke all regulations and did not even strap on my equipment and revolver, but just went down the communication trench followed by the others. No sooner had we arrived than a shell fell plumb on the post and buried all our equipment and would have buried us. We had to return later and dig our stuff out.

One night my platoon was digging a trench about 100 yards in length. Suddenly the Germans dropped a series of crumps, as we called their 5-inch shells, right at one end of this trench line. You don't feel like going and standing where the shells have just dropped with their acrid smell, but something said to me, "Move over from where you are standing (at the other

end of the trench) and go where the shells have just dropped."
I did so, and a moment later the next set of crumps fell
exactly where I had been standing.

My closest escape was in the bloody, muddy battle of
Passchendaele in 1917, when we British lost a quarter of a
million men in the attempt to dislodge the enemy. It had
rained solidly for all the early days of August, and by the
middle of the month the place was a sea of mud, pocked with
shell holes, where men sometimes drowned if they fell in with
their heavy equipment, and where we could only travel safely
on duckboard tracks. The advance was very slow. We had
taken one German trench line with deep, well-equipped dug-
outs. But naturally the Germans knew the exact range.

I occupied a good dug-out with my company commander,
Ratcliff by name, and I second in command. We were in an
inner compartment with two wire bunks, and a thin three-
ply-wood partition separated us from the company sergeant-
major and about eight men of the headquarters staff with him
in the outer room. There was intermittent shelling. In the
morning I was stretching out my hand from my bunk to get
a tin of bully beef for breakfast when there was a sound, not
like an explosion, but like a sheet of metal being rubbed
against another sheet. The dug-out was filled with smoke and
the partition had fallen on top of us.

When we got out, we found all the nine men in the other
room lay dead in a heap. It had been a direct hit on them.
Later that day, during which we remained properly shaken, I
even found, as I unrolled my raincoat, the little finger of one
of the men which had somehow been blown into it. Why
them and not me?

A few days later, we went over the top to capture an
objective about a mile ahead of us. I lined my platoon up at
3.45 a.m., and in my last word to them I spoke of what it
meant at such a time, when few of us might return alive, to
have received Christ as a personal Saviour. I wish now that
I had spoken even more emphatically to them. We then had
a prayer. At four-thirty the whole sky was lit up as the tre-

mendous barrage of hundreds of guns opened up behind us at zero hour and the shells went screaming over our heads on to the enemy lines, and we followed behind as the barrage moved forward. But there were evidently groups of Germans untouched in their cement machine-gun shelters, and I saw the section of men on our right mown down and lying in a heap. We went a little farther forward, across a small muddy stream called the Steenbeck, and then crouched down awaiting the lifting of the barrage to a more distant objective.

I was in a shell hole with my batman and several others. There was the staccato sound of a machine-gun and I saw my batman change colour. A moment later he was dead and there was a stain of blood on his tunic hear his heart. That was all. But the next moment I felt what seemed like the sharp blow of a stick on the back of my leg. A bullet had penetrated, shot from behind. It must have been from some machine-gun emplacement we had passed by that was now at our rear. The bullet had entered above my right knee and made its exit a few inches higher up. It was bleeding quite a bit and I could not walk too well. So as the advance continued, I gradually limped my way back, using my batman's rifle as a support.

As I passed further groups, making their way up to the battle by the duckboard tracks, they would call out, "Lucky so-and-so, got a blighty." That's all it was: but after being bound up at the forward casualty dug-out, I was put on an ambulance and we bumped our way back to further treatment; and this led to the hospital ship across the Channel and the hospital train in England.

II

God's Plan and His Partners

HOW MUCH TURNS ON HOW LITTLE. THAT IS WHY I ALWAYS SAY to young people, Just see to it that you are occupied with doing God's will for the present. He has the future in His hands, including the exact purpose for your life. I personally had no idea what I was going to do with my life. I always had the background conviction that just as the front line was the only possible place for a young fellow when his country was at war, so to take the Gospel to those who had never heard of Christ was the Christian's front line and I ought to go there. But I had no sense of direct call, and was therefore rather thinking of either taking a permanent commission in the army, as I have already said, for I liked the life; or alternatively of taking up teaching in one of our public schools. My earlier ideas of getting ordained had faded, as I had come to the conclusion through my army experiences that you got down to fellows where they really are better as a layman than as a parson.

My disappointment was when our hospital train passed through London, where we all hoped to be detrained, and went on to Leicester in the Midlands, where they had turned a large mental sanatorium into an officers' hospital. Yet my whole life's call and career hung on that. I hadn't been inspired by the various padres, as we called the chaplains in the battalion. They didn't seem to want to co-operate in witnessing activities, or themselves to be out to get the fellows to Christ; though now I realize that my own youthful zeal lacked the charity which could have sought co-operation with them and perhaps given them encouragement in their difficult padre's job.

Anyhow, I hadn't been long in my hospital bed in Leicester

before a chaplain walked through the ward, and at once I seemed to sense something different about him which attracted me, something of Christ in his face. We soon got acquainted, and I learned he was Gilbert Barclay, who had a parish in the north in Carlisle, where I had a great-aunt who turned out to be a leading light among his people. So he brought his wife Dorothy to see me, and I learned that she was a daughter of C. T. Studd.

I hadn't remembered hearing of him before, so ignorant was I of famous names in the Christian world; nor did I know, till my mother informed me, that not only was he notable, but that he had four daughters who were spoken of as the "four beautiful Miss Studds"! And that out of the four the three older ones were married. Still less did I know that Dorothy, having looked me over, had written to the unmarried one, Pauline, and told her that there was an eligible young man in hospital here and she might come up herself and have a look. Such are the female nets laid for the unwary.

In case there may be some who know nothing of C. T. Studd, when he and his family are to be so much part of this story, I will give this brief outline. C.T., as he was commonly called, was one of three famous cricketing brothers, all three captains of Eton and then captains of Cambridge in succession. C.T., as a cricketer, was by far the greatest of them. While still an undergraduate at Cambridge, he was twice officially named as the best all-round player in England for the year. Their father, a wealthy man, was brought to Christ through D. L. Moody, and the change was so great that a visiting evangelist at their large country estate was able to lead the three boys separately to Christ on the same day. At the height of his cricket career, a crisis brought C.T. to an act of total commitment of his life to Christ, when love of cricket had begun to choke his love for his Saviour. The result was, after winning several of his all-England cricketing friends to Christ, he heard and responded to the call to inland China as a pioneer missionary.

48

Six other Cambridge men joined him and they became known as the Cambridge Seven, the most notable missionary band ever to leave Britain for the mission fields. Their going opened the floodgates to a surge of volunteering for missionary service by university students which has never ceased since. They went out as members of the China Inland Mission. While in inland China, Studd heard news of the sudden death of his father and that he was an inheritor of a sum of money equivalent these days to about half a million dollars. Responding to what Jesus had said in the gospels to the rich young man, he gave the whole of it away in various amounts to different agencies for the spread of the gospel, stating in his joking way that anyhow the Bank of Heaven was safer to rely upon than any earthly bank.

After ten years in China, he and his young wife and their four daughters returned to England through ill-health, just escaping the Boxer massacres. Some years were spent in travelling among colleges in Britain and the U.S.A., then a further ten years in India; but as he was still troubled with asthma and signs of T.B., they were back in England, apparently with their missionary careers ended. However, the missionary fires burned as ever, and, though he was now over fifty, a sudden challenge came to him for the heart of Africa. He seized on this, despite warnings from the doctor and the fact that his wife had become a semi-invalid through heart trouble, and with no human backing and empty pockets. His answer to critics became the motto of the Crusade he then founded: "If Jesus Christ be God and died for me, then no sacrifice can be too great for me to make for Him."

Long ago he had learned to put total confidence in "the Bank of Heaven", and so he started out alone. The word he wrote back to his wife from on board ship became the divine commission and driving force of what is now the Worldwide Evangelization Crusade (W.E.C.): "God has spoken to me in strange fashion and told me that this trip is not just for the heart of Africa, but for *the whole unevangelized world*. To human reason it sounds ridiculous, but faith laughs at impossibilities and cries it shall be done."

It took him six months to reach his "El Dorado" in the exact centre of the continent, the N.E. Belgian Congo, and there he started reaching the multitudes he found in the forests. This was 1914, and the outbreak of World War I prevented more than a handful of reinforcements joining him. Mrs. Studd had got off her sick bed by faith and was going around the country calling on young men and women to join this baby mission.

Something then happened of revolutionary importance in my life, and which may indeed have been a factor in Dorothy's letter to Pauline. Gilbert, passing my bed one morning, quite casually dropped on it a little magazine called *The Heart of Africa*. It contained the accounts of C. T. Studd's penetration into the then Belgian Congo, opening the first mission centre of this infant new mission, which he called "The Heart of Africa Mission", at Niangara, the geographical centre of the continent. It wasn't the geography or location which captivated me, but his glowing accounts of the crowds of primitive Africans who were giving him such an uproarious welcome. No sooner had I begun to read than as clear an inward voice as ever I heard in my life said, "That's where you are to go." I had received my life's call and knew it.

I wrote to Mrs. C. T. Studd in London where she was using their home at No. 17 Highland Road, Upper Norwood, as an office and recruiting centre, telling her of my call and sending a donation, though still not knowing of the daughter with her.

But I escaped that net of Dorothy's. Before Pauline arrived for the inspection, the army had transferred me south to a convalescent home in Bournemouth. However, Mrs. Studd was the heart of hospitality, and had invited me to come up and stay with them whenever I could get to London. About two weeks later, while I had begun to move about on crutches, a summons came to attend an investiture by King George V at Buckingham Palace to receive the Military Cross from him. So I came and stayed with Mrs. Studd.

Here I received a shock and enlightenment on a false idea of mine. I had thought from my little experience with the girls I had met that beauty and non-Christianity went together, and Christianity and non-beauty. Till I met Pauline. My fate was sealed, and the net closed on me the very next day when travelling up to the Investiture. Pauline had a war job in a London office, but as we travelled in the train together she began to tell me about what the Bible teaches on Christ's Second Coming. So ignorant was I of my Bible and its contents that I had not heard of this and realized that I was with a very beautiful girl and one who knew more of the Lord than I did. I was done for.

The Investiture was exciting, my only visit to the interior of the Palace, and I was especially surprised when as the King hung the medal on the small attachment on my tunic and asked me about my wound, he ended by shaking hands and saying, "Pleased to meet you." I thought only commoners talked like that. I appreciated his courtesy.

But naturally the ultimate outcome of that train journey was more exciting. A girl-friend of Pauline's had travelled down with us and she told her afterwards that what was going to happen was obvious and inescapable. It happened on the evening after Armistice Day, November 12, 1918. I asked Pauline to come down to London, have dinner with me and then we would tour around and see the celebrations of the city gone mad with relief and victory.

When we reached a dark corner by the Obelisk on the Thames Embankment, I really hadn't meant anything so drastic, daring and final, but having held her hand (as well as her arm) and with the excuse of steering her through the crowds, I sort of felt I must go all the way. As a good reserved Englishman, I had never even used her Christian name before; so, feeling ice-cold within and terrified, I called her Pauline, told her I loved her and was there any chance. The immediate reply was numbing, "No, it can't be."

51

But I was quickly to discover that in her abysmal modesty she had got things the wrong way round. She meant, "No, it can't be that you want me," which is what I should have said to her, and have said ever since.

Her mother graciously consented, and her father away in Congo had no alternative but to accept the son-in-law dumped on him.

CAMBRIDGE AND KESWICK

Demobilization followed in January 1919. Meanwhile Cambridge University had made a very generous offer to any who had been going up with a scholarship or exhibition before the war. They could come for a short four-term course and be granted a pass degree. It must be understood that the pass degree at Cambridge is very simple and really elementary. Anyone with a reasonable educational background could get that. An honours degree is a very different thing. Probably, if my mind had not gone to seed through the five years of war, I could have gained a second-class honours, and even that is not a mean attainment; but with that entirely out of range and at my age of twenty-four, I was glad to accept these easy terms. As the whole Studd family had been at what I would say is the leading College of Cambridge, Trinity (where Prince Charles, the Prince of Wales, has entered), I was able to transfer to it.

It was a great year for me. In my last months before demobilization I had been attached to a training battalion as bombing officer at Maidstone, Kent. We were billeted in homes in the town, and I had the offer of two homes. One was Warden House, the beautiful home of Mr. and Mrs. Frank Fremlin. Fortunately, a Christian friend in the town had mentioned to me that Mr. Fremlin was an active Christian, and so I asked to be billeted with them and their daughter; and fortunately for me, after I had called to see them, they accepted me.

It was the beginning of a lifelong friendship. The old couple have gone to be with the Lord, but Margaret, their daughter, still remains among our closest friends. They moved to a lovely home in about 20 acres of beautifully kept gardens and grounds near Tunbridge Wells, called Rusthall Lodge, which became a home from home to us through the years. It was Mr. Fremlin who suddenly said to me, when walking together in Maidstone, that if I liked to go to Cambridge, he would pay for it. Later, it was they who supplied all our equipment and passage money to go to Africa; and later again, when I was planning to write the life of C. T. Studd, arranged for me to be alone in a farmhouse on the Scottish moors (where, indeed, for many summers they sent us as a family).

He once wrote to us in Africa and told us to let him know whenever we had a need. It was a temptation to accept; but as I will explain later, we did not feel that that would conform to the faith principles upon which the mission worked. But again and again through the years, they helped us with gift upon gift, as well as the lovely hospitality of their home.

I had also come to a final conclusion that my attempt during war years to mix certain habits which are usually considered as an indication of love of the world rather than love of God, smoking, drinking and dancing, with my witness for Christ, was detrimental. They had not got a grip on me except that I did like smoking; and though I had sought to use them as a point of contact, it seemed to me that, because I was doing those things, those of my fellow-soldiers who did profess to accept Christ probably thought that they could do the same just for the love of them. It may have prevented them from the clean cut which by one means or another is a necessary step in a separation from the world and a total committal to Christ. At least it seemed to me that nearly all those who had accepted Christ in my army contacts dropped back again, and I attributed it to this. So on Armistice Day, as the victory sirens were sounding, I threw my tobacco pouch into a ploughed field and that was the last of it.

I do not mean by this that I judge all those who don't make the cut off I did. I know dedicated witnesses to Christ, who love people and reach down into their needs more than I do, who continue with some of these things. These outward practices are to me matters of individual judgement and guidance, and not standards for one to impose on another. However, for myself and my life's calling, I am sure I did what was right for me and God's will for me.

I am afraid Cambridge did not mean intellectual development for me. I don't mean that that should be normal for a normal student. But we were not a normal crowd of undergraduates. A great many of us were ex-officers, from colonels downward, with an average age of twenty-four rather than nineteen. For myself I chose theology and geography for my subjects. But I soon got a shock in theology. As I have said, my Bible knowledge was extremely superficial. I really only knew Christ as my personal Saviour and had been a bold witness for Him, and had read my Bible as any keen young Christian would do.

My theology was Bible-based in a simple fashion. I took the position, which I still do, that if I accept any of the Bible, I accept all, and the Scripture-based faith of Jesus and Paul was my foundation also. Where there are passages I cannot understand or explain, I prefer to learn lessons from them for my own living rather than question their accuracy.

My tutor's instructions at Trinity were for me to attend the lectures of Dr. Charles Wood of Queen's. But he soon shook me badly. I found his main occupation seemed to be to explain away the Old Testament miracles one by one; not to show us by what means we could profit by or learn lessons from these incidents, but how they must have some naturalistic explanations—and that was all. The end came for me when we reached Elijah getting the people to pour barrels of water drawn from the brook Kishon over the sacrifice on Mount Carmel, before the fire of the Lord fell and consumed it. Charlie Wood carefully explained that this brook was an oil well and that while Elijah had the people praying, he ignited the liquid.

After that I asked permission not to attend any more, but

54

to take my exams on the basis of private study. My tutor did not seem to mind, obviously recognizing that the so-called studies of us ex-soldiers were largely farcical. And to prove my point, when the results of the first part of the exams were announced, I was in the first division! Again it will be understood that to be in the first division of an exam for a pass degree is a thousand miles away from the first division of an honours degree!

But this lack of necessity to take my studies seriously meant just what thoroughly suited me. I could throw myself into seeking to win men for Christ as zealously as in army days. For years Cambridge had had an evangelical Christian union which had first come into being in the days of a famous old evangelical university preacher, Charles Simeon. It was given the name of the Cambridge Intercollegiate Christian Union (always known as C.I.C.C.U.—Kick-You). It owned a very nice little hall in the centre of the town known as the Henry Martyn Hall (named after the great missionary scholar to Persia) where the daily prayer meetings were held. But through war days its numbers had dwindled to about a dozen, though it never went out of existence.

Now there were a few of us men back who had taken our stand for Christ in the services, Godfrey Buxton, Murray Webb-Peploe, Clarence Foster (though he was never in the army for conscientious reasons), Clifford Martin, Charles Bradshaw and others. The numbers soon began to increase, and others were added, as we gave out invitations, until we were thirty, forty, fifty meeting for those grand half-hours at 1 p.m., of a hymn, Scripture and few comments, and then down on our knees with no gaps between the praying, for God to work by His Spirit on many hearts.

But we were soon faced by a problem and challenge. There was a much bigger and more popular Christian Society in the university which had world-wide connections, the Student Christian Movement. We both had special Sunday evening services, the C.I.C.C.U.'s in the evangelical Holy Trinity Church, with special preachers and the aim being to bring

one's friends and get an opportunity to talk with them afterwards about a committal to Christ. But the S.C.M. did
things on a much bigger scale. They invited down men with
famous national reputations, such as Lord Horne, one of the
best-known generals in the war, and Lloyd George, the Prime
Minister. Of course, they had large audiences, but we knew
that the speeches made, while they might have a Christian
and ethical emphasis, would by no means be aimed at directly
making men face their lost condition and the necessity of the
new birth.

One of their leading sponsors among the dons, however,
Charles Raven of Emmanuel, who talked of a conversion
experience he had in the trenches, was conscious of how much
the S.C.M. lacked the spear-point of the direct challenge, and
that this was just what we C.I.C.C.U. men had. Would we
not join them as their kind of shock troops? The then
C.I.C.C.U. president was Daniel Dick, and I was secretary.
So it was arranged that we met the committee of the S.C.M.
in the room in Trinity Great Court of their secretary, Rollo
Pelly. We did this; there were about ten of them, and we
two. After an hour's talk, I asked Rollo point-blank, "Does
the S.C.M. put the atoning blood of Jesus Christ central?"
He hesitated, and then said, "Well, we acknowledge it, but
not necessarily central." Dan Dick and I then said that this
settled the matter for us in the C.I.C.C.U. We could never
join something that did not maintain the atoning blood of
Jesus Christ as its centre; and we parted company.

It did not mean that we don't know many men with
S.C.M. connections, from their great founder John R. Mott
onwards, who are devoted servants of Christ, and there are
occasions when there can be some kind of combined witness;
but we took the line then, and have continued it ever since,
that for ourselves and tens of thousands of others likewise,
loyalty to the Christ of the Scriptures, and the Father who
sent Him, and the gospel which, by Paul, is traced back to
and squarely based on the faith of Abraham, "the father of
us all", demands of us an acceptance of the inerrancy of the

Scriptures; and that once doubt is cast on them as our foundation, the crack which may start by appearing tiny can end by a crumbling of the whole structure. By 1 Corinthians 15:1–6 we stand.

This really set the C.I.C.C.U. going again on its old foundations, and from which it has never moved to this day. I was unable to participate in physical activities; my football knee, and then the wound in the same leg and consequent operations, had put me out of count for these, so I had my afternoons free. I decided that I should seek to give a witness to every man in my college, Trinity. I hated and dreaded the idea. I knew that for the most part Trinity men were from the wealthy or top families in the nation and would likely be supercilious. Men such as Anthony Eden, the future Premier, were up at that time. Each man had his own room. Trinity had about nine hundred men, though only part of them would be living in college. So I went to each man's room, knocked, always hoping there might be no reply, and often there wasn't, and if so I would just leave a C.I.C.C.U. card of invitation to the meetings. But when there was, I handed the man the card of invitation and added a word of what Christ meant to me personally.

I can't tell of much result of these visits, but I do know of one. The captain of the college tennis and soccer, and one of the top mathematicians in the university, was an undergraduate named Carey Francis. With special fear I knocked at his door. He was in. I handed him the card and said much the same as to the others and left. A year or two later, when I was in Africa, I heard that Carey Francis was now a witness for Christ and a don at Peterhouse College, Cambridge. So when I came home on my first furlough I visited Cambridge and called on him.

I caught him just going out to a lecture. He did not recognize me at first, but when I introduced myself he burst out laughing and said, "Well, when I last saw you, I don't know who was most frightened—you or I. But after you had left, I said to myself, That fellow has something about his faith in Christ that I obviously don't have. I had better look into this." And as a result, Christ not only found him, but Carey later left his secure position in Cambridge to start a high school in Kenya for the better education of picked Kenyans.

So great was the influence of that school that nearly all the men in the present Kenyan Cabinet are alumni of it, and when Carey died recently, though an Englishman, all his pall-bearers were cabinet members or in big government positions, bearing their tribute to what he had meant to them, and always with Carey it was a Christ-centred education.

That summer the Keswick Convention was restarted. It had always been a custom for there to be a Cambridge Camp for undergraduates. This could not be arranged, but Mrs. Studd with her usual generosity offered to run a house party. Twenty-eight came, including a few from Oxford, one being Noel Palmer who, 6 feet 8 inches in his socks, naturally went by the name of Tiny Palmer. He had been a wounded officer in a Cambridge hospital, but as he knew some man in Christ's College, we met in his room and the spark leaped from the one to the other. Tiny found Christ, which ended by him starting up in Oxford an Oxford University Bible Union. This later became the O.I.C.C.U. (Oxford Inter-Collegiate Christian Union) which is as strong in Oxford today as the C.I.C.C.U. in Cambridge.

About halfway through the Keswick Convention, one or two of us felt that God was not yet at work in our student house-party as we believed He should be. So we gathered that evening for what we thought might be half an hour's prayer. One man, younger than most of us, too young to have been involved in the war, was among us—Hamilton Paget Wilkes, a son of that God-used missionary to Japan, Paget Wilkes, of the Japan Evangelistic Band. He let loose in prayer, and I had not heard a person storm heaven like that before. There were no inhibitions, and he was out beyond self-consciousness. We were still there at 2 a.m., but by this time a strange thing was happening to us, strange at least to me; the burden was lifted for God to break through in power in our house-party, and we were sitting about in all kinds of positions and laughing as we praised. What we had sought for was done. Of that we were certain.

The next few days proved it. It was as if the atmosphere had changed. It was not a question of one man trying to change another. God was there doing it, some out in the fields by themselves, but the house-party was set on fire, and men made acts of dedication which have lasted through a life of service. We were so "intoxicated" that we went out nightly arm in arm along the road (it was a fine week, unusual for Keswick!) singing our way to a copse by the Lake. Our favourite chorus was "Grace fathomless as the sea, grace flowing from Calvary, grace enough for you and me, grace enough for me." I am afraid we overdid it, because we had complaints for being too noisy, but men on their faces in that copse came through to God.

"Praying through" to assurance like that was new to me. My young brother Kenneth, with his brilliant mind, was going through a period of professed atheism, and my godly father was appealing to us all to pray for him. I went out by myself and did so until I had that assurance, and then boldly (perhaps brashly) wrote and told my father there was no need to pray any more. His conversion was a certainty. That was July. In September we were both home.

There was a dull little weekly prayer meeting at the church, attended by a few old ladies. Anyhow, I thought I would go, when Kenneth suddenly said he would go too. I did not know what to think of that—it was surely the last place for him! At the prayer meeting something seemed to grip me to let my heart out and pray for the stirrings of the Spirit and conversions in that little town of Parkstone, near Bournemouth, where we were living since my father had retired. That was all, and we went home.

Next morning Kenneth came into my bedroom and said he had not been able to sleep because God had spoken to him at that meeting but when he responded to God, He had said to him that it had to be all or nothing. If he was going to give himself to God, it must be the whole of him. And he had done it. How much has poured out of the Spirit to the Church of Christ, especially the Church of England, from that midnight transaction.

MY SISTER, DR. VIOLET, AND BROTHER, SIR KENNETH

Kenneth was the youngest of us four children. The four consisted of my elder brother Harold, to whom was added the family name of Crichton-Stuart; then I came with the extra name of Percy after my father; then our one sister, Violet, called also Margaret after Mother; and then Kenneth, with the second name of George after my father's favourite brother I have already mentioned, so greatly used of God as a clergyman-evangelist.

My brother Harold and I were very close in our youthful days, probably through the wisdom of our parents sending us to separate public schools, which meant we really enjoyed each other in the holidays. He went to Haileybury College. But our paths divided when Christ became real to me as my Saviour, and he later said that our friendship was spoiled when I became a religious fanatic. Harold's life never blossomed into anything effective. He was at Jesus College, Cambridge, and gained his M.A. He did well in World War I as a staff officer in the signals, and being twice decorated, with the Military Cross and Bar.

He came out of the army with a damaged heart and on government pension, and, after trying various jobs, he finally settled as Tourist Agent in Switzerland for Frames Tours during the summer months, and lived his bachelor life in South Africa during the winters. He never married. He died quite suddenly at sea through his heart condition. For some years he professed to have no faith, but in later years he stated his preference for the evangelical type of service and used to attend the Cathedral in Cape Town. Mother, therefore, always hoped there were the roots of a redeeming faith in him.

My sister Violet has been the real wonder of our family. I have never known her anything but the loving servant of all. From early years at home, it was always she helping Mother when we were playing around. My grandmother, who helped to pay for our schooling, held to the Victorian philosophy that boys must have good education for their future, but for girls this was less important. So while we went to expensive boarding-schools, Violet had to go by bus and bike to the Bournemouth High School for girls, an excellent education under a Miss Beale, I believe, and probably just as good as ours, but without the old school-tie aura.

But in addition to my grandmother's help, even in my thoughtless youth I remember catching the sense of the sacrifices my parents made for our education, Mother spending hardly anything on clothes for herself. Violet reminds me that when she graduated from Westfield College in 1921, "I asked mother with much trepidation whether I could have a new dress for the graduation dinner (I had no money of my own) and she had to say no; and then added that in the last few years she had never spent more than £7 a year on herself and had not had a new dress all that time, and just could not find the money for a graduation dress."

Violet gained a scholarship to Westfield College, a women's college of London University, and another one in her first year there. Having gained her B.Sc. degree and five years later a Doctorate of Science of London University, she went to China as the only English teacher on the staff of a very special Chinese school for educated girls of high-ranking families, under Miss Tseng, a member of one of the great Chinese aristocratic families, and an earnest Christian. She went as an educational missionary attached to the Church Missionary Society. Five years later she returned to England to the staff at Westfield.

One of England's most noted Headmasters, Sir Cyril Norwood, had a very high opinion of her and after some years he, as chairman, offered her the appointment of Headmistress of Westonbirt School for girls, a large boarding-school, housed in a magnificent mansion and park in the Cotswolds. Here she was eminently successful for ten years, taking the school through war days where they were moved to Bowood, the family mansion of Lord Lansdowne. Violet's influence in the school was always that each girl should find the basis of true character and purpose in life in the lordship of Christ.

Finally, she felt she would like to give her remaining years of teaching to the training of teachers; so she resigned Westonbirt and accepted an appointment as Principal of the Salisbury Teacher Training College. Before her retirement in 1962, this college nearly doubled its numbers and was honoured with a visit of the Queen Mother to open the extension building.

Our bond of intimacy and love has increased through the years. Violet is good for me, having lived her life in a wider Christian circle than mine. We might find we differ on some minor Biblical interpretations, if we dug into them, but I have been too busy enjoying the richness of our fellowship in Christ and interchange on many subjects in which we are deeply at one. Fellowship with her is a thrill I always look forward to.

Kenneth, the youngest of us four, joined Violet in appropriating between them the major part of the family inheritance of brains and brilliance. From a boy he had unusual capacity for the absorption of knowledge. He would take Father out and ask him to point to any constellation, and he had the name for it. He could quote reams from the poets. He took up the study of yachting while still at school, and one of the masters who was himself a retired naval officer told me that Kenneth knew more of navigation than he did.

I have already mentioned his conversion, in so far as I was connected with it, though he would have much more to add if telling of it himself. This was followed by his call from God to the mission field in the same Mission as myself, but his was to the Indians of the Amazon. He was the first to produce by intense investigation a map of the known tribes of the Amazon basin, which was standard in the early twenties, and subsequently a volume explaining the linguistic clarification of two to three hundred tribes.

During this time and later, he made several journeys as a pioneer missionary in which he barely escaped with his life, especially in a visit to the Parentinlin Indians 500 miles up the Madeira Tributary of the Amazon and 1,000 miles from the sea. Other journeys of extreme risk took him through the great rapids to the sources of the Amazon up the Huallaga and Ucayali Tributaries, and other forest journeys through to Bolivia, Colombia, Peru and Venezuela. He wrote books on these travels, such as *Amazon and Andes*; but vivid writing was not his strong point, and I hope he will now, when nearing his retiring years, write much more of those dramatic travels.

Becoming known as a missionary expert on those northern regions of Latin America, and with his knowledge of Spanish and Portuguese, he joined the staff of the World Dominion Press as a survey editor. He also contributed to *The Times* for Latin America.

When clouds were gathering in the late thirties, which presaged coming trouble with Hitler's Germany, Kenneth was secretly recruited to become a member of a skeleton Ministry of Information under Lord Perth. When war was declared, this Ministry was officially established. Kenneth was quickly promoted from being in charge of the Latin-American branch of the department to being in full charge of the Overseas side of the Ministry under Brendan Bracken, who was Winston Churchill's Minister of Information. He was made a C.M.G. (Companion of St. Michael and St. George) for his services; and for travelling purposes to give him freedom in planes and so forth, he had privileges equal to rank of Major-General.

After war days, rather than accept an offer to join the Foreign Office or take a leading position in business, he returned to serving the Lord in a more direct way by accepting the honorary appointment of President of the Church Missionary Society, the main missionary agency of the

Church of England, which he held for twenty-five years. He was also one of the founder promoters of the World Council of Churches, and has remained a member of their main Committee and head of their Commission for International Affairs. More recently he has been three times elected as Chairman of the House of Laity of the National Assembly of the Church of England. He is the first ever to have been re-elected a third time in succession, and the first evangelical to hold this position. He received the honour of Knighthood from the Queen.

Kenneth has never moved from his roots in Christ, and the main objective of his life has been to be a witness for Christ. God has used him to reach men most of us could not contact, and I am sure his influence has contributed to the recent up-surge of evangelicals into the Church of England ministry, where today the evangelical training seminaries are filled, while the others have a shortage of recruits.

Many, especially in the U.S.A. where things are always seen more as black or white, often regard such agencies as the World Council of Churches as wholly apostate. It is notable that when we get nearer to the heart of them, as I have been able to a small extent through Kenneth, we find that God has His Christ-centred men among them, even though the directions in which they seem to be going in many respects may arouse our opposition. Having been close in fellowship with Kenneth during the years following his conversion, we drifted more apart during the years of his rising to the top: but more recently we have drawn together again, and enjoy meeting, corresponding and praying to-gether.

Kenneth's first wife, Eileen, was in Amazonia with him in our W.E.C. She died suddenly through pneumonia and pleurisy, a great blow to him. His second wife, Nancy, has been just the one to be beside him in the strains of his responsibilities, for she has been a rock of strength to him in his normally nervous disposition. Their four children, two of Eileen's and two of Nancy's, are grown up now, and we have mutual interest in our two families, and in some helpful links where sometimes uncles can get a rapport with nephews more easily than fathers!

Kenneth has maintained close association with Billy Graham from his first visit to England, and has been a much-valued member of his British Committee.

A recent and amusing outline of his life, as interpreted by the secular press, was published in the *Guardian* of July 4, 1968, accompanied by a cartoonist drawing. It says:

Man of the Church

If any single person can claim to be the Church of England, it's assuredly Sir Kenneth Grubb, who moves among the bishops like a sleepy whale amid codfish. Chairman of the House of Laity, President of the Church Missionary Society, Chairman of the (ecumenical) Churches Commission on International Affairs, he's now—at 67—shedding the last two offices, just as he's graciously shed most of the 48 committees to which he was once said simultaneously to belong. But then, Grubb's life has been a constant series of planned retirements. He ran away from school at Marlborough. He had a period as an evangelical missionary in the Amazon hinterland, spending four months alone (after the murder of his party) with a rifle and New Testament. During the last war he joined the Ministry of Information as Latin-American expert, swiftly became Controller of Overseas Publicity, and applied himself to the job with true evangelical ruthlessness (when Rommel was advancing into Egypt, all the astrologers had been bribed to predict a great British victory). As a chairman he's much sought after and claims to act on a plan; but experienced ecclesiastical observers reckon he really gets by on a blend of no-nonsense piety, strategic craft and impromptu instinct.

THE FIRST INTER-VARSITY CONFERENCE

Back now to Cambridge. When we went up for the Michaelmas Term, we carried on as at Keswick. A few of us "prayer addicts" would meet in a man's room for afternoon tea and then get down to it, often for three hours at a time on our knees, for God to break through at the University. In those days Cambridge was a men's university, and the two women's colleges were on the outskirts of the town—well away— Girton and Newnham. It was only about that time that Cambridge got far enough to grant degrees to women, even if they had passed all the exams! But we also voted against having women at our C.I.C.C.U. prayer meetings. I shall surely be thought an anachronism when I still say I think it was good. It kept us down to what we were after without distractions!

There was one far-reaching answer I do know of personally, to our labours in prayer. Alfred Buxton, who had gone out with C. T. Studd to start the work in the heart of Africa, and had married Edith, his third daughter (Edith has just published a fascinating description of what their early life meant for those four girls in the Studd household, and then in Africa, called *Reluctant Missionary*[1]), was home on furlough and urging the need of immediate reinforcement for the exhausted little band of six who had stuck it out in Congo through the war. Should I go on now? I had only two more terms—from January to June of 1920—to get this pass degree offered on a platter by the University, and I knew I could easily do that; and then by the strange Cambridge custom, all you do in two or more years is to pay £30, and your B.A. becomes an M.A.! Not an easy decision.

It was attractive to wait the extra half year and get the degree. Sometimes in my human pride I still regret that I didn't. But no. I know now that God had something bigger in store if I obeyed, and I decided to go at the year end. That meant leaving the University in November. And this was what God had in store.

I don't know how it came to me like this, but I felt convinced that, before I left, I should go round all my friends or acquaintances with whom I had some links of friendship (though not the inner circle of my keen C.I.C.C.U. friends) and I should pull no punches. This was the last time I would see most of them, and I must tell them exactly what my inner convictions were about how they stood with God. To me it

[1] Lutterworth Press, London, 1968, and Christian Literature Crusade, U.S.A.

was something like Elisha suddenly equipped with the spirit of Elijah. Obviously not a thing you can do under ordinary circumstances, and normally it might be well considered presumptuous and judgemental. But I did it, and it was a breakthrough.

I had seen nothing like it before, for we had all found Cambridge with its sophisticated ex-officer caste tough to break into; but man after man, some sixteen of them, faced up to the need of accepting Christ, or getting something right which was a block. It was a revival on a small scale and the C.I.C.C.U. asked me to have a special meeting with them about it, which I did.

But the outcome which really mattered was a sudden flash which I can only call an inspiration. If God was working like this at Cambridge, and there was a small start at Oxford, should not every English university have a Christian Union, and then out to the universities of America and the world? Why not have an Inter-Varsity Conference in London as a start? I shared my vision with two friends, Clarence Foster, who in later years was the greatly loved and honoured Secretary of Keswick and head of the Scripture Union, and Leslie Sutton, who has had a major part in the founding and development of Lee Abbey, which has been such a spiritual power in the Church of England.

We agreed together that this was of God and we would get going in arranging this conference around Christmas. We gathered other interested men in to pray and plan it, using Charles Bradshaw's large room in New Court, Trinity, close to the rooms now occupied by Prince Charles. The result was the first Inter-Varsity Conference (I.V.C.), with a good group from Cambridge and a few from Oxford, London and Durham. That was all. But it was the beginning of what has now actually spread to the ends of the earth.

The I.V.C. continued annually until, under the leadership for years of Dr. Douglas Johnson, who has really been God's man in developing the I.V.C. to what it is today, it was changed to the Inter-Varsity Fellowship (I.V.F.). Howard

Guinness carried the torch into Canada, Australia and New Zealand; Stacey Woods established I.V.F. throughout the U.S.A. but using the extended title of I.V.C.F., adding the word Christian; and in more recent years Stacey Woods has expanded the I.V.F. into the I.V.F.E.U. (Evangelical Unions) which has its unions, and groups, or chapters all round the world in hundreds of colleges and universities.

It is always a thrill to me that I was given a hand in the start of the I.V.F., and that it was the outcome of obedience in dropping the degree, which anyhow in real value was worthless!

A BROKEN ENGAGEMENT—REMADE

But I was going through the mill in quite another way during those last six months at Cambridge. Maybe there is a fanatical strain in me, but when I began to learn what kind of man this C. T. Studd was, his own way of sacrificial living and the standards for those who joined his mission, of which I will speak in more detail later, my heart went all the way with him. Pauline, on the other hand, had felt through the years, in ways I never had, the sting and slur of being a child of parents who lived "by faith" when the other members of the family were wealthy. So Pauline was not so enthusiastic about the "selling out" life at that time (though through the years God has made us absolutely one on it). The consequence was there was some reaction when I would talk enthusiastically about living with only one suit (not that in fact I ever have!).

The final crisis came, after she was already disturbed by some of the far-out things I said, when in the spring vacation I had a chance of spending a week on a caravan with the Open Air Mission, but chose instead the prospect of a week in Mrs. Studd's home. While travelling down to London, I foolishly read a book which is like a red-hot poker to someone on stretch for God—Charles Finney's *Revivals of Religion*. It was as if a loud voice was telling me I was rapidly losing out by loving someone else more than God. So disturbed was I, and I suppose so unwise, that I carried my doubts and questionings to Pauline. The result was a beckoning finger next day to go into the dining-room with her, where she gave me back the ring. That did really kill me. No pleading would change her. She said "for ever", but she also said that I finally asked her to let me know if she ever changed her mind. I didn't remember this. But I know I went into the most agonizing few months of my life. I (we) had been so sure that our engagement was of God, and we were so sure, and really knew it, of our love for one another. How then could I reconcile this?

I had one friend, Alf Byne, who had been a fellow-officer and a bold witness for Christ. He said, with no uncertainty, that he wasn't going to take this break. God meant us to be together and He would bring us together again. Not another hopeful voice in the darkness. I really suffered, because I did not know in those days how to suffer, yet still accept suffering as coming from God with a purpose of love; so I did not know where to find a faith that could make an adventure out of adversity, and thus have a peace and praise which could swallow up the pain.

Back in Cambridge I hated to burn her letters, but I did; and in the summer vacation, spending part with my loved Uncle George, how often I hopelessly paced the park in an agony near their home in Highbury.

But there is no easy way for the vibrant human self to die to its own clamant self-desires and find a resurrection in which its sole desire is God, and its human joys can be taken or left according to the measure in which they further the love-purposes of God for the world.

With the prospect of marriage gone, I did not see the importance and significance of the test which now came to me. My Uncle George who loved the Lord with all his heart and had been so greatly used by Him, was of a gentler mould than C. T. Studd, and C.T.'s soldierly and sometimes sporting or slangy language and call for a sword-in-hand attack on the lethargy of the church did not appeal to him. So with this break with Pauline he tried to persuade me to join a little mission in India which he said he knew would take me. It was tempting because Studd's mission was so small, and I faced the fact that if I continued to go out to him, I might well have as my next-door neighbour some more fortunate person who did win and keep Pauline's hand; and I already had my jealous eye on one or two possible prospects! Why not cut loose and build a new life elsewhere? But there was still God's call, clear and unmistakable—to C. T. Studd and the heart of Africa. So I turned my uncle's offer down. I did not realize that when the Studd family saw that I was sticking to my call and preparing to go out at the year end, they began to say to Pauline, "Why be so foolish? Look, he's still going forward with us."

And there was something else. God began to deal with Pauline. She later confessed to me that when she turned me down, she had said to herself, "If I marry that man, I shan't even be second in his life. God will be first. God's work will be second, and I third. And I'll be third in no man's life." But the final stroke was God's own strange way. For some reason when she accepted me she had a text from Scripture, Philemon, verse 15, where Paul wrote about Onesimus, "Perhaps he therefore departed for a season that thou shouldest receive him for ever." As this came round again in the daily reading, this time she was caught in the net; she had better obey the word; and I say she did the proposing to me! At least Alfred wired me to meet him in London, and when I arrived, told me that Pauline was awaiting me. I had a last qualm. Was I after all meant to remain single? But that was the last. If I had not married Pauline, and had her sane anchorage in my life, the Mission would surely not be in the God-blessed shape it is today, or I should have been long out of it in some far-left field.

We married on November 24, 1919, with a company of the C.I.C.C.U. men to wish us God-speed, and Noel Palmer with his vast bulk for me to hide behind as my best man. The C.I.C.C.U. gave me a wrist-watch inscribed with "From the CICCU, Hallelujah". We felt it in keeping with our soon

70

departure to the Congo to cut out the usual wedding trimmings. Pauline wore a simple blue travelling dress and I a blue suit. On December 24 we sailed for the Congo, with one other who has been a sister to us through the years, Lilian Dennis.

But these six months had meant a real death to claiming any human rights to each other which could take precedence over what God wanted for our lives. Our love has remained the permanent basis of our lives. We have had all the human joys of a God-blessed union. She has been to me all I could wish her to be. We are both strong-minded and, although we recognize the husband as the head of the wife and household, I have a far bigger opinion of her wisdom than of my own, and we have always acted as a partnership and not as one bossing the other. But there have been occasions when after long consideration I have still felt some way God appeared to be leading me to the right one, and I have taken it; but very rarely without us both coming to see alike about it. We often differ and battle things out, and that is healthy. She is always plain with me about myself, which is also very healthy for me. It has meant very many partings, as I will explain later; the amount we have been apart must add up to a third of our lives I should think; but that original dying to each other gave us a freedom to go God's way, though at cost, and it has never once been easy for either of us to be apart from the other. Perhaps it is a good thing when major clashes of outlook can be resolved, as ours were, before we married; and I think it saves a lot of trouble and heartache. We did die to each other as having a prior claim on each other even in our married lives, and it has been as Gilbert Barclay quoted for us in his marriage talk from Ecclesiastes—Two are better than one; but a three-fold cord is not easily broken.

71

III

To Congo with C. T. Studd

C.T. WAS RIGHT, AND WE WERE WRONG

I AM NOT GOING TO WRITE IN A DETAILED WAY ABOUT THE Mission with which we have spent our lives, first called the Heart of Africa Mission, and then enlarged to the Worldwide Evangelization Crusade, because I have already written much about it, and this is a book of personal reminiscences. The book which has had the outstanding circulation is the life of *C. T. Studd, Cricketer and Pioneer*. Without exact statistics (some were destroyed at the publisher's by a fire-bomb) I should think it has reached a combined circulation of a quarter of a million in some fifteen languages. Probably readers of these memoirs have read it. It has had a tremendous impact on thousands of lives, and still after thirty years I continually meet with those who were almost exploded into a full dedication through it. There have been other books and biographies also—*After C. T. Studd*, the story of the developing Crusade, the life stories of *Alfred Buxton, Jack Harrison, Edith Moules* and others. But I will only talk of the work as it relates to my own experiences.

I shall for ever be thankful that God called me into a missionary crusade based on these principles. I am as sold on them now after forty-nine years as when I first joined. To be part of a crusade to the whole world has always had a satisfying appeal to me. To have as its sole aim what we officially call "evangelization", in other words, the one objective of bringing Christ to people and people to Him, still remains for me the highest calling in life. The name "Crusade" preserves that fighting, daring, self-dedicating attitude to the calling which was so essentially C.T.'s, and comes out in those little booklets which he wrote soon after arriving in the heart of Africa and which were considered the greatest challenge to missionary dedication in the early years of this century—*The Chocolate Soldier, Christ's Etceteras, For the Shame of Christ, The Laugh of Faith,* which are still in print. So the title "Worldwide Evangelization Crusade", though clumsy and difficult to repeat, does give the full flavour of what we exist for.

The two main principles of the Crusade equally appealed to me—sacrifice and faith. Sacrifice was obvious. If it is your privilege to offer your life that others might have eternal life, you expect God to take you at your word and that it will cost your life—whether that takes forty days or forty years. Faith had always appealed to me ever since in earlier days I had read the life of George Muller and how he built and provided for his Bristol orphanages by looking to God alone without making his needs known to man. And this had been followed by Hudson Taylor, the founder of the China Inland Mission, with whom C.T., as a member of the famed Cambridge Seven, had started his missionary life in China. So when I saw that C.T. had founded this Crusade on the same faith principle, it rang the bells with me.

Pauline and I had between us about nine hundred pounds, which had been what we soldiers called "blood money"— a government remittance according to rank and length of service on leaving the army. We decided we would spend this on our missionary needs, travel, etc., until it was exhausted, and then there would be the promises of God. As our friend, Mr. Fremlin, financed our first outgoing, it was a year or two before we came to the end of this "nest egg". But we had our early shocks of other kinds in plenty, on our arrival on the field, though not on the principles of the Crusade. How good for us, although we did not think so then.

Our journey out was the normal one for those days, taking three months, by ship to Alexandria, then by train and river boat to Khartoum; then the real adventure of penetrating the heart of Africa starting by two weeks on the little flat-bottomed river steamer with a stern-wheel right up the winding Nile to near its sources. Fascinating, passing villages of the long-legged Nilotic tribes, Shilluks and Dinkas, standing like herons with one leg bent up against the knee of the other (and to think that now there are many churches among them, and I believe the first Dinka Bishop); continually watching the lazy crocodiles on the sandbanks with their toothy mouths wide open while the little white birds picked their teeth; the hippos showing their fat noses above water and diving down again; once a herd of about two hundred elephants which, when the steersman blew the ship's whistle, raised their trunks in the air like one man and thundered off into the grass; sometimes the long thin neck and head of a giraffe peering up above the tall grass.

At Rejaf we disembarked, and were carried by truck 100 miles to the Congo border. Across there, met by one of that little band of missionaries, we started the 300-mile journey by foot and bike, with porters carrying the baggage, first through days of grassland, and then sighting the long thin line of the beginnings of the tropical forest which would be our home, stretching for maybe 1,000 miles to the south.

These are the usual type experiences of the earlier travellers, and the way we lived through the twenties. Our shocks did not come from these. But we had acquired a sentimental idea of the "dear heathen", with some built-in really wrong notions of a crowd of black saints awaiting us.

At Nala we met with C.T., Pauline's father, my father-in-law, whom I then saw for the first time. In himself he was all that we expected, in his loving welcome, the old aristocrat now accustomed to living the African way; always scrupulously clean, in simple khaki shirt and shorts and stockings, with his long beard and somewhat bent frame, aquiline nose and keen piercing eyes. His home was a stoutly built mud house, originally built by a Belgian official, with his bedroom on one side, and an open centre where we sat, had our meals and small meetings, all surrounded by beautiful palm trees in their hundreds.

But we were ill at ease. Without realizing it ourselves, we

had been the petted and pampered "fine young Christians" in the homelands, and now we were going out (even the Executive Committee told us that!) to bring help, refreshment and encouragement to the tired little band in Congo. Tired little band! They were not looking for any to bolster them up. All they wanted were some more fellow-soldiers! We found C.T. had no time for special welcomes and favours for a daughter or special preference for a new son-in-law. He stood where Jesus stood, "Who is my mother or my brethren? Whosoever shall do the will of God, the same is my brother, my sister and mother."

I think, without recognizing it ourselves, we were puzzled and hurt that we did not get any better reception than any other new recruits. There was no let-up with this man—no diversions, no days off, no recreations. The zeal of God's house had eaten him up, and souls were his meat and drink.

But what shocked us most was his attitude to the professing African Christians, five hundred of whom would gather on a Sunday morning. Where we had been told to expect a concourse of shining saints, C.T. was saying that sin was rampant, and nobody who continued in sin entered heaven, no matter how much he was supposed to have been born again; and that he doubted, holding up the fingers of his two hands, whether ten of these five hundred would really get there. We thought this awful. Our theology was thin enough on any count; we had never had any Bible training, but we had picked up the usual evangelical teaching that once a person was born again, no matter how he sinned, if once in grace, always in grace. He could not be unborn. C.T. took no count of that. His stand was "without holiness no man shall see the Lord", and a person living in sin, unless he repented, no matter what his past claims to grace, he would be outside heaven. That shook us. There were Scriptures for "once saved, always saved", but there were Scriptures on the other side also.

C.T.'s strongest critic was the greatest pioneer of those early days, James Lowder by name, who single-handed pene-

78

trated the Ituri Forest to the south and met with such a response from the tribes-people that that whole area later
became our richest harvest field. But doctrinally he was at
opposite poles to C.T., and accompanying us on our journey
in, even before we had met C.T., he sowed the seeds of these
questionings in my mind, fertile soil with my feeble Bible
foundations. Later, as with Paul and Barnabas, "the contention was so sharp between them" that he left the work.
Years have now passed, and James Lowder, now in his
eighties, lives in Miami, and we have maintained friendship
by occasional visits, for nothing can ever take away for me
the greatness of his pioneer daring and the greatness of the
fruit of it. But at the time he strongly influenced me towards
his point of view. This was good for me. It made me search
the Scriptures until, after years of consideration, I have come
to take a middle line.

There are the Bible assurances of being secure in Christ.
There I personally live without a shadow of uncertainty. But
I don't ask that the Bible should be a systematic theology to
suit my theological mind. Revelation through the apostolic
writings was a string of unsystematic letters, written existen-
tially to meet some church need of the moment; and in them
I also find plain statements about the dangers and possibili-
ties of falling away. Why should I be more systematic than
the Bible and Paul and the other apostles? Why must I be
bound by the frowning looks of the majority of evangelicals
if I don't wholly subscribe to their pet convictions? If I drive
a car, I don't live in fear of an accident; but there are occasions when crossing a road I look around to see if it is safe.
So to me the Bible does give many plain warnings, and I can
go along with C.T. in this, that though living in the eternal
security of being sealed unto the day of redemption, it is "a
fearful thing to fall into the hands of the living God" in a
condition of blatant disobedience.

It was a good thing for those simple believers just rising
out of the morass of heathen superstitions and sin to be
brought up straight against the facts of sin as sin; and C.T.

never had any remedy for sin or the possibility of living a new kind of life except the Blood and Spirit of Jesus. The very intensity of this gospel of holiness that he preached and lived, even going to the extent of cutting off any water baptism or partaking of the Lord's supper for ten years, when he found that many were hiding beneath these as supposed means of salvation, is undoubtedly the firm foundation to the holy Spirit-filled church in Congo today which, if he was alive, could now be said to be his "joy and crown".

It was true that C.T. was never one with whom it was easy to discuss or maintain an opposite point of view. What he saw to be truth was truth to him, and that was that. C.T.'s soldier virtues, sword in hand for God and against the devil and sin, did make him, doubtless unrealized by himself, one with whom it was uncomfortable to disagree.

Pauline also had never been the daughter he was closest to. He teased her in childhood and often reduced her to tears in those younger years, and put, I believe, something retiring into her nature. The other three, especially Edith and Dorothy, were of the more sporting type dear to his heart. Strange that in his last years he should be landed with us two as his successors. God's ways. Yet, neither Pauline nor I had ultimate difficulty, or at least not after certain earlier battles had been fought and won, in standing along with him in the fierce oppositions of some of the missionaries, his own home committee and in the end the Christian church in general. We had settled the matter that we all have sides of our nature in which we are unacceptable to some and could well do with improvement; but God is with those who stay in the battle lines, no matter how "ornery" they may be; and C.T. was one of those. While others criticized, left, attacked, he stayed on where the fight for souls and a Spirit-filled church was at its fiercest, and we decided that that was where we should be too.

But we did have troubled years. Before long we both tried our hands at "improving" him and got our fingers burned. I went to suggest that if the church was in such a low state,

why not have some special prayer meetings for revival?
"Surely," he said, "but I don't believe in praying in work
hours. Let's have a meeting at 4 a.m." (work and activities
starting at 6 a.m.). "But," I said, "that is the time when we
get up to have our own quiet times. When shall we have
those?" "Why not earlier?" was the answer. Next morning
I was up at 4 a.m. for my own quiet time; but across the compound I heard the old man's banjo going. He had gathered
a 4 a.m. prayer meeting of some of the Africans. I did not
attend!

Pauline tried her hand by suggesting that she might take
over the running of his domestic household. "Thank you,"
he said, "but Mama Mototo" [one of the women co-workers]
"does it very well."

Finally, I think he saw that in our conceit and self-
assurance, and indeed criticism of him, we needed a good
lesson. So he suggested that we go out about 25 miles and
occupy a newly opened station, beautifully situated on a hill
called Deti, from which in the early morning you can look
out over miles of palm-filled forest and see spirals of smoke
arising in the still air from the many villages; and equally see
the fierce tropical storms approaching. We knew enough of
the simple language used as a lingua franca among the tribes
of that area—Bangala.

C.T. had shown wisdom in concentrating his attention on
this market language, poor though it was, because by it we
could at once reach many tribes, the men in the main knowing
it. It meant interpretation in village meetings; but that too
had its advantages, when we had tried Christian interpreters,
because they could often put in more intelligible language
things we were trying to say in more Western forms. C.T. has
been justified in standing against criticisms from other missions in the use and development of this language, because it
is now the officially adopted language for the whole north
Congo.

In those earliest days we also had another significant
little indication that God speaks more through warm hearts

than critical minds. Lilian Dennis, who, as I said, accompanied us to the Congo, is a nurse but no linguist. But she had a heart filled with love for God and the people, and was far more mature in the Spirit than we youngsters were. She only had the language very roughly in those first few months, whereas I was able to get along fairly well. So I would speak at the Sunday services. One Sunday morning when I was away, it fell to her lot, doubtless with fear and trembling, to have to speak both morning and evening. In the morning she spoke very haltingly on "I will, be thou clean". The elders came to her afterwards and said, "Mama Deni, what you said so reached our hearts that we would like you to repeat it this evening." I never had that said to me!

So off we went to Deti. We were soon trying immature experiments. The Africans loved the bits of western clothing they could get hold of, and they were their Sunday best. Well, we also had nice European clothing. But we thought it much better if any African Christians who went out to take the gospel to the villages should dress in their native barkcloth, a rough garment made of the bark of a certain tree and worn round their waists. They rebelled. We insisted. We soon had things in chaos, and where a few hundreds had been coming to the meetings, we were reduced to around eighty. Then God spoke to us. "Go back and humble yourselves and just be learners. Your father has forgotten more about leading people to Christ than you ever knew." So we wrote, confessed our pride, apologized and got all the loving welcome back he could give us.

THERE IS A "SECOND BLESSING"

But God was using these tensions for our own lasting benefit. A friend of Pauline's, Dr. Isa Lumsden, was sending her a little paper called *The Overcomer*, published by Mrs. Penn Lewis, well known in England as a Bible teacher. But what she wrote about didn't make sense to us. She was not speaking about Christ dying for us, but of our being crucified and dead with Him, and risen with Him. That was all new to us.

At first it didn't register much with us, except that we felt there was something there we hadn't got hold of yet. But our need was great. We had heard others at Cambridge and other places speaking of knowing that you are filled with the Spirit, especially Barclay Buxton, the father of Alfred, whom we undergraduates were fond of getting down to talk to us. Pauline and I knew that we had no such inner witness, and we desired it. We had one canoe journey to do for some days on the Aruwimi River, a tributary of the Congo, stopping at villages every now and then on the banks. I spent the intervening hours studying a commentary on Romans by an American, I think Stifler by name. Light began gradually to dawn on the meaning of this identification with Christ in His death and resurrection.

Finally, we were out for a visit to a dear and zealous African brother, Bangbani. He was the only light in his chiefdom, and what a welcome he gave us to his little plantation, throwing his well-oiled arms around us so that we came out of the embrace looking like zebras. That night he gave us his best, his cook-shed, with a few banana leaves strung around for privacy, and our two camp-beds in it. The equipment we brought to the Congo and which was our house furniture was a canvas camp-bed each, with mosquito net, a canvas camp table and chair, enamel plates and cups, and cooking pots. That, besides our clothing, which for us men was just khaki shirts and shorts, with stockings or puttees week in and week out—very sensible and comfortable—was the main part of our living necessities.

But when Bangbani left us we could not go to bed. The full moon was out and it was all quiet in the banana plantation except for the usual chorus of insects, with the moon shining between the great banana leaves. So we took the two little camp chairs and sat outside in the moonlight. There is not much trouble with mosquitoes in that area. We had decided together that we would wrestle this thing out with God, and specifically claim then and there that we should be filled with the Spirit. It was only later that we got our theology more in line—to discover that He in His fullness had always been there—His Spirit joined to ours, since we had been born again: and that what we needed was not a filling from outside, but a witness borne to the existing living relationship. We took Galatians 2:20 to be the fact by faith: "I am crucified with Christ, nevertheless I live: yet not I, but Christ liveth in me" and we went to our camp beds around 4 a.m., having accepted the matter as settled by faith. We awoke no different; but I took a postcard and drew a tombstone on it, and wrote "Here lieth Norman Grubb buried with Jesus". Probably we all have to get settled on the reality of this death experience before the resurrection can be uppermost in our consciousness. At least that was the period I was in.

Nothing further happened to me in relation to this for a couple of years. For Pauline, it was different, and she tells how a few days afterwards, when sleeping alone in a native hut, the hut was filled with a consciousness of His presence and a voice confirming to her that their union relationship was fixed for ever.

Two years later I was at home and visiting this same Mrs. Penn Lewis whose little magazine had first awakened our interest. I had gone to her to talk over our perennial problem of tensions on the field, but I think she must have observed that beneath this I had my own need, for instead of talking about the problem she told me what happened when she had been "baptized with the Holy Ghost", as she called it, and the power of God had come on a group of young people she talked with that night. As she talked, it was like a great light lit within me, bringing the inner awareness which has never left me since, of Christ living in me; and living in such a sense that it was not I really doing the living, but He in me, in His Norman form. The Scripture against which I had written my name and date that next morning in Bangbani's village had become permanently alive to me—this great Galatians 2:20.

There was a great deal I had not yet got into focus; those clarifications had to follow later; but one tremendous fact had become fact to me, and the passing years and deepening understandings have only underlined it as the fact of facts—that the secret of the universe, and the key to my own life, is simply the Person Himself in me; as Paul had put it, "The mystery hid from ages and generations but now made manifest to His saints . . . which is Christ in you."

I had been drawn to and sought an answer before in "holiness teaching", especially through Barclay Buxton at Cambridge, and from him and others I had caught it that there is an inner fixation, a settling in by which we can know that we are not only born of the Spirit but filled with the Spirit, and which I knew I did not have. But I had some mistaken ideas. I had thought that I myself as a human would be made holy, and thus not respond as before to irritability, lust, pride and so forth; that an actual change would take place in *me*. I had tried this way, taken it by faith that this "entire sanctification" had become fact in me; but it had not worked. These same things continued to make their appearance in me. But now I was seeing something different. My humanity did not change.

I had to learn later that it is not meant to change, because every potential of my human nature is there to be an agency by which Christ can reveal Himself. Sin is not my various faculties or appetites, but shows itself in the misuse of them, when they are stimulated by temptation into action in a wrong direction, and I wrongfully struggle, as in Romans 7, to overcome what independent self can never overcome. It is the independent self which is the sin principle, for independent self is and can only be self-loving, therefore I am helpless in myself to resist the stimulation. But, another Self, God Himself—Father, Son and Spirit—has now so become the centre of my being that I am merely the vessel containing Him. Now, knowing this, my attention is no longer centred on myself, the vessel, and fighting against my fears or depressions or what not and expecting change in myself, and disappointed and condemned when it doesn't happen. No, I accept myself. The vessel doesn't change, but it contains Him, Christ living in me, joined to me, Spirit with spirit.

It is the same idea as when a room is dark. We don't centre our attention on the darkness. The darkness is not wrong, unless it is misused; we accept it but don't struggle against it; we just replace it! We look for the switch and turn on its opposite—the light. And when the light is on, where is the darkness? It is swallowed up. It is there in the sense that it appears immediately again when the light is off, yet it is not there to my consciousness with the light on. So now this awareness of Christ in me is the permanent switching on of the light, and the permanency is the importance. I now live in a new consciousness. At any time I am temporarily conscious of temptation which can lead to sin, but that does not mean that He who is the light has gone from my inner centre. He is the permanency; and the appearance of Him being not there, and of me being in the dark is an illusion. I have been tricked into moving back from eternal reality to temporary appearance. The change is in my consciousness, not in the fact.

So I learn to live by the repetition of recognition, which is the practice and habit of faith. He in me is the all, the joy, power, wisdom, victory—all. I transfer my attention, my recognition, my affirmation from the human vessel to Him whom it contains: and that is switching on the light; and the light swallows up the darkness; yet the darkness was needful to give manifestation to the light. And when I do fall into a sin, which I do, the forgiveness for all sins was pronounced from Calvary two thousand years ago, therefore the forgiveness was there before the sin, and I can boldly appropriate that.

So this had become the central fact of our lives—Pauline's and mine—which has to become so in every life—call it by what name we like—the Second Blessing, Entire Sanctification, the Baptism of the Spirit, the Fullness of the Spirit, the Second Rest, the Exchanged Life. We can only live by what becomes part of us, not by something imposed from without and clung to by us. In the new birth, Christ has become real and personal to us as a Saviour, the Spirit has borne inner witness with our spirit that we are the children of God. So again in this second realization, Christ has become known to us, not merely as the Saviour from our sins but also as the One who is living our lives. Then it was His righteousness in place of my sins; now it is His Self in place of myself. This actually took place at the new birth, but, for nearly all of us, we cannot yet see deeply enough into the roots of our problems, which is our self-reliant selves, to be conditioned to see Him as the Divine Self living His life through our human selves. We have to go through our "wilderness" experience, all of us, redeemed but still regarding Him as separate from us; and we seeking to live the new standards of Christian living as best we can, but with constant failures, self-disgust, strains and stresses we cannot handle. We had a first collapse when we recognized our guilt as lost sinners and came to Him for salvation. We have a second collapse when, now redeemed, we discover our helplessness. First we had learned we *had* not done what we should. Now we learn that we *cannot* do what we should. And so, as after the first collapse, we were conditioned to see and affirm His blood replacing our sins; now, after the second collapse, we are conditioned to see and affirm Himself replacing ourselves.

And the way into the full realization is always the same, the only way of faith, just as Pauline and I found, when in faith without feeling we took our stand that night that Christ does live in us; the same as years before as a young fellow I had taken it by faith that my sins were no longer there, because He had borne them for me. Faith, always faith alone. But the process of faith is that if I take a thing, it takes me, and I know it has taken me. If I eat food, it takes me over and I know it afterwards. So when I take Jesus by faith, I become conscious that He has taken me. Faith has never become a completed faith until there has been this reflex effect; for "faith is the substance of things hoped for, the evidence of things not seen". In this way in my case two years later, and in Pauline's only two weeks later, our act of faith had its inner confirmation.

I think that is why these days so many have found confirmation for their act of faith in the experience of speaking with tongues. It was evidently the confirmation given at Pentecost, also with Paul, and if it was the common experience in the Corinthian church it was likely to have been so in the churches of that day. Confirmation that He does live in us in His fullness, as I say, is the inevitable outcome of faith. When the confirmation has come by the experience of tongues, I thank God for those to whom He has confirmed Himself that way.

I also recognize that for many of these the experience is so satisfying, releasing and indeed overwhelming, that in their enthusiasm it is easy for them to take it for granted that none have the fullness of God who have not spoken in tongues; and some can be embarrassingly insistent on this and proselytizing to the point that it causes division. But there is no Scripture authority for such an insistence. We all would like others to share in the good things we have, and that is natural; but to insist on tongues as the necessary evidence of the fullness of the Spirit goes beyond the teachings of Paul and the others, and is an error.

I am one who naturally responds to anything which appeals to me as emotionally satisfying or heart-enlarging or personality liberating, and I have often felt that my friends who have the tongues-gift have much I could benefit by. I admire and thank God for them, and I have at times gone to God about it. But to me the answer comes clear that it would be a step back, not forward, to seek a manifestation when I have the Manifestor. Having been made certain that He with all His gifts is the total Vine of which I am a local branch-expression, my calling is to be myself expressing the Vine-life, Him Himself, just in the ways in which He spontaneously expresses Himself by me. The All cannot be limited to one form of expression, even as Paul and Peter make plain when they list some, and I believe only some, in Romans 12,

1 Corinthians 12 and 1 Peter 4, of the varied gifts of the Spirit.

So I congratulate all who have manifest gifts I have not, but I must not for myself be diverted from my simple abiding as branch in the Vine, and the fruit is the business of the Vine. It may well be that a gift of the Spirit, such as tongues, is experienced as an additional release of the Spirit in a Spirit-filled life. This is something to be thankful for, so long as, through immaturity, it is not wrongly confused with being a necessary evidence of being a Spirit-filled person.

But I do see one thing. I am sure there are many redeemed people who, as I was, have not moved into the fixed and final act of faith that Galatians 2:20 is the fact in their lives, or in whatever way they may verbalize to themselves their inner eternal union with God, and He the One living their lives. Or, if they have, it does not seem real to them, and they doubt whether they really have. But having once taken the step, the fact is the fact without any inner consciousness of it. Even the desire for an inner witness we have to die to, for it is a final form of self which wants to have for itself. *I* know. *I* want to know. And that very desire to know is the final form of unbelief, because it means "I am not really sure and need to know." So faith needs to take its stand on fact, and not even by inner witness: "If I make my bed in hell, Thou art there."

Yet it is the changeless law of faith that what we take takes us; so when we no longer finally hang the validity of our faith on the need of knowing, by some means we shall become inwardly and fixedly aware of the Union. When we no longer seek the awareness (the witness), we shall have it, because then we are safe from immediately turning it into a final form of self-exaltation: "Now *I* know." After we have ceased to seek the awareness, we shall have the awareness.

To both Pauline and me this experience stands out in our lives as next in importance to when we found Christ. We have never been able to shrug this off, as I often hear people do when some mention is made of "the second blessing", by adding that it is only one of ten thousand blessings. No, to us, it was and is "the second blessing", if we call our new birth "the first blessing"; and the two stand by themselves as mountain-tops in our life's experiences.

A CHEQUERED FEW YEARS

This did not mean the fights were less fierce, but we had begun, only begun, to know how to fight with effective weapons. I spent a lot of my time in the bush, visiting the villages, getting the people together and seeking to explain the gospel to them. I was always very much at home with them. There was considerable response and small village congregations would begin to meet together regularly. They had no written language and therefore depended on hymns which C.T. had written and they would memorize, or smatterings of the hymns they picked up.

I won't say much of those years because ours were the normal experiences of young pioneer missionaries in the days when our means of transport were foot or bike, and the women missionaries were carried in hammocks. Our calling as a mission has always been concentration on bringing Christ to the people by direct evangelism, and building the believers in the Spirit-filled life. Everything else has been secondary. Because of total illiteracy we started simple schools, and have occupied ourselves through the years in translations and dissemination of the Scriptures and books that help in Christian living; we have regarded the spread of the written Word equally as primary evangelism. We have also ministered to their bodies by simple medical assistance through station and bush dispensaries, also in leprosy work; but we saw in the Scriptures that the first world missionaries, Paul and his co-workers, immersed themselves in the one work of preaching the gospel and building up the churches in the Word and the Holy Spirit, and this has remained our pattern.

We see that the uniqueness of the Gospel is that when He who is self-giving love takes over a human life, the one who is taken over himself becomes an other-lover, and not just blessed but a blesser, not just healed but a healer, not just loved but a lover; so we have realized that giving human assistance to those who need it, better education, physical healing, better living conditions, wholly misses the mark when it meets these needs but leaves the recipients as much self-lovers as before. The betterments merely enlarge the opportunities for self-advancement. Compassion must meet need. Jesus did; but with Him, as with us, while this was an inevitable expression of love, His heart and purpose were set on something far different—the production of a race of humans for whom the meaning of life had become not to have their needs met, but to meet the needs of others, and to meet in them their greatest need which would make them in turn the lovers of others. And this is the gospel.

In 1923 we came home. It had not been an easy baptism into the mission field. We had our first son a year after we had arrived on the field—Noel, named after Noel Palmer. There was no doctor within several hundred miles, and our loved Ma Deni (Lilian Dennis) helped Pauline. The little fellow was a good boy and seemed to go ahead until he began to teethe; but then he took a turn the other way, no one could tell why. Too late to take him the long journey (all by foot), he slipped away from us on his first birthday. I was out at a Christian Chief's, Mofoi, about four hours through the forest, and travelled back through the night. We laid his little body under a group of palm trees, a rough box for its resting place, lined with cotton.

A big crowd gathered for the first death of a white baby. One little African boy came to ask if black boys could also go to heaven. Under Ma Deni's tuition he became a notable Christian and witness right up to his early death through pneumonia, and his life story became a booklet much used in home meetings—Fataki.

Pauline began to show signs of anaemia, and we were able to take her the long journey to Aba, the headquarter station of our brother mission, the Africa Inland Mission, where she received much kindness and treatment from their Dr. Woodhams. It was originally diagnosed as pernicious anaemia, but her recovery seemed to prove it was not.

While with her there for some weeks, I tried my hand at translation, starting with an abridged *Pilgrim's Progress*. This was a success, and led on through the next five years to the translation of the New Testament, and parts of the Old. According to Bible Society regulations all missions using this trade language, Bangala, had to be consulted, and they were five in number. But the final decisions were left in my hands as the translator, though I worked especially closely with my old friend, Harry Stam, of the Africa Inland Mission. Twenty thousand was a first edition, but it went on to further editions of many thousands until the time for a full revision came, and the completion of the whole Bible.

I have already said how wisely I think C.T. was guided in centring our efforts on the development of this simple trade language. How many tens of thousands hear the word of God through it who might still be waiting for translations in their own dialects. I deliberately kept it simple so that bush villagers would not be stumbled by mysterious phraseology. But even then I made mistakes. Years afterwards I found I had used a word for "answered" which really meant "denied"; I noticed how intelligent African readers skipped the word when they were reading "Jesus answered and said", and that is how I found the mistake.

From then on till the thirties our lives became very chequered. Pauline stayed at home. Our second son, Paul, was born soon after our arrival, and a year later our daughter, Priscilla. But the call was still the heart of Africa, and so we decided that if there must be some separation, it must be between us rather than between us and the children. I had not been at ease when asked to speak at home. I had seen very little which seemed to me plain evidence of changed lives. I was in the stage of being more exacting and critical of the response of the Africans, than understanding, hopeful and loving. At the same time I had not yet learned to be dead

honest when speaking at meetings, and was always wanting
to present a glowing report. The result, of course, was strain
and forced talk. I have surely had to be forgiven for many
exaggerated stories. I think it is one of the hardest things for
a missionary to be dead honest!

So back I went to the Congo. I did not find those separations easy. We usually counted a spell on the field to be five
years and we separated, prepared not to see each other for
that length of time. But, maybe deliberately, C.T. kept
sending me home to represent his points of view to the home
committee. Twice I left Pauline to stay five years, and twice
it was not more than a year. I got plenty familiar with that
leisurely journey down the Nile.

The Committee had become restive with C.T., partly
because of some of the resignations, and partly because they
had the idea that, as he had said in the beginning that God
had called this Crusade into being "not only for the heart of
Africa, but for the whole unevangelized world", he should
take more active interest in opening new fields. But C.T.'s
answer was quite simple and plain. He had gone to Congo
because God had told him to go. His job now was to see
Africans saved and filled with the Spirit. When it came
God's time to call others for other lands, let them go ahead
as he had done.

I am sure he was right in this, and not the Committee. It
kept the basis of the Crusade on God's individual calling to
this one or that, not on a Committee "sending" them. And
when a person responds to God's call, without influence or
support from men, then he will carry through his calling
on God's resources, not man's. Thank God C.T. kept us
free in this way from Committee management, and on
this basis all the world advances of these years have been
made.

I was with C.T. all the way in what he stood for, and when
it came to a choice, in the fierceness of the conflicts between
the Committee points of view and C.T.'s, I was with C.T.,
because he was the front-line soldier fighting the battles,

while they were the stay-at-homes; and I believed God was more with the fighting men. To this day I think I was right, and time proved it. But my difficulty was the sharp sword with which C.T. seemed to write, rather than with the pen. He fairly laid it on, and in this respect I was more a man of peace than of the sword. So it tore me apart having to return to present these kinds of dispatches to the Committee, agreeing with what was written in essence, but not in manner of presentation.

On one such return visit it was only Pauline with her sense of honour which kept me from throwing in the sponge. Alfred Buxton had parted company with C.T. with great sorrow of heart. Instinctively I was more one in spirit with Alfred, and, while I was at home representing C.T. to the Committee, Alfred suggested that together we start a new venture in West Africa. How glad I am we didn't. I don't think either of us had what it took to found and build a pioneer work. But when I was wavering and much attracted by the offer, Pauline came down on me like a ton of bricks. She said, "You came home as Father's ambassador. An ambassador is honour-bound to report back to the authority who sent him. You cannot in honour run away like this. You must go back, tell him how you feel, and then do as you like." Good words! I went—not to a favourable reception when I tried to make clear that I agreed with him in principle but not in the wording of it. C.T. could not accept a separation between those two.

But how wise is God. C.T. had already told me that when I returned he planned pulling back from field leadership and putting me in. But now he called the missionaries in and I was on the carpet. I went about for a day or two with no one speaking to me. This was the time when, whether right or wrong in my viewpoints, I had such a marvellous realization that it was not I, but Christ, in going through this. Of course, the others obviously thought the same about the position they were taking. Well, that is just the strange thing about God and us; we can violently disagree on opinions, and yet

God can be on both sides where the hearts are right as they see it.

Things quietened down, because at bottom I was still with C.T. and the field, and not with the Committee; but from that time on C.T. began to groom for leadership one who had become like a son to him—Jack Harrison. Jack, who was from the poorest areas of Liverpool, was the very opposite in background from C.T., yet what a man of God he was and became. I had the privilege of writing both their lives, and the contrast is enormous; but I still think the ideal standard life for one joining this Crusade is the life of *Jack Harrison Successor to C. T. Studd*, showing just what God can put into and get out of a young man with practically no earthly advantages.

But at the time, when I could see Jack being chosen instead of me, I had a battle with inner jealousy. But not for long. Again how wise is God. I simply was not cut out to be a field leader, and to bring that wonderful growing African church of Christ to its adolescence, as Jack did. On the other hand, this break seemed to free C.T. to see that leadership at the home end might be God's place for Pauline and me; and that turned out to be God's plan, as much as Jack for the Congo Field.

Not long after, C.T. called me in and said plainly that he wanted me to go home and take our place there with an ultimate view of leadership. That shook me, because I had never backed down on my call to the Congo. At first I said I couldn't, and for that reason. But C.T. quietly reminded me that our Principles and Practices lays down obedience to our leaders. So he kind of implied it was that or . . . I spent a day with the Lord, and then there came clear to me that what I had really always so liked about the W.E.C. was its world-wide calling, and that if I was part of a world-wide W.E.C., I should be willing to take any share in it which seemed the right one. And so I complied and once more returned home. This was 1928.

C. T. STUDD THE STORM-CENTRE

Pauline and I were to visit the Congo once more together and see Father once more. Mother Studd, that heroic woman, had built up the home with the constant pain in her heart of separation from her husband. She saw him for the last time on a suddenly planned visit with a friend to Egypt, and C.T. rather reluctantly (feeling that at her age she couldn't take the journey too well) sent me to fetch her from Khartoum. She had two weeks with him and then I escorted her home, and soon after she went to be with the Lord.

But it was obvious to us, after her death, that opposition to C.T. was mounting at home and that at his death, when he would no longer have a veto as founder, the Committee were already preparing to moderate the mission. They felt there was an extreme in his standards of sacrifice, faith and holiness for the churches which should be toned down. Pauline and I were aware of this and greatly concerned. It was obvious also that we ourselves were being put in a backwater where we could not have too much influence on things, though on the Committee.

Our concern became so great that we suddenly said to each other that we believed God would make it possible for us to go out and visit Father once more; but we knew that that would not meet with his favour unless he had invited us. Within a few days a letter came (we corresponded frequently) in which he said he wished he could see us. So there was the open door and, I forget how, the fare was also provided. We arrived in the autumn of 1930, and when we got there, he asked, "How did you come here like this?" "Because you asked us," we said. "No, I didn't," he answered; and we produced his own letter! He was delighted because he knew the seriousness of the situation.

Then the blow fell. The Committee had heard that we had told him what was going on. They called me a "fox in pants", and dismissed both C.T. and ourselves from the Mission. They had their good reasons. They had been

Norman Grubb and Pauline Studd on their wedding day,
November 24, 1919

With my brothers-in-law, Gilbert Barclay and Alfred Buxton,
and "Mother Studd"

shocked because a while previously C.T. had written a book-let called *D.C.D.* Concerned whether we should lose our standards of all-out dedication, he had asked in one of his evening sessions with the missionaries, how would a British soldier describe his loyalty in war-time. Someone said he would say he didn't give a damn for anything except give his life for his king and country. "Well," said C.T., "and I want to be one of those who doesn't care a damn except to give my life for Jesus and souls." *D.C.D.*, Don't Care a Damn. When published in booklet form, it shocked most people in Eng-land. It sounded like swearing. But again they too easily forget that the man who said this was doing it, while the critics were in their safe spots in the homelands. So once again I and those in Congo with C.T. were with him in this and declared ourselves DCDs along with him; for the way he lived meant more to us than the way he worded it.

In addition to this, another disturbing fact reached them at home, and that was that when having one of his bad bouts of fever, a passing doctor had given him a shot of morphia which had immediately revived him. Finding this a remedy for his quite frequent attacks, which we think turned out to be more gallstones than fever, he asked his friend, the well-known missionary doctor in Uganda, Sir Albert Cook, to send him some morphia tablets. This Sir Albert did on several occasions, saying that actually C.T. should return home, but, knowing he wouldn't, these would keep him going. Once or twice these packets were brought in by visiting missionaries without declaration because of difficulties which might have been raised. With this news reaching the home, and that he was taking this morphia to enable him to get up and continue his preaching activities, and the way in which once or twice the pills had reached him, the Committee decided that the only thing to do was to remove him from the mission, and us as his assistants, and thus free them to remould as they wished.

I can see their point of view and there was much reason in it. But those on the field with him and we two from home, knowing what God was doing in African lives, and that C.T. had no other aim in life but to continue to bring Christ to them, stood with him, and if he was dismissed, we were all dismissed.

It being obvious that he would not long be with us, he asked the missionaries to choose a leader among them. The unanimous choice was Jack Harrison; and at the same time they commissioned Pauline and me to go home and go straight forward with the original call to W.E.C. for the world; and in opening new fields, we were not to regard them or hold back in case it might divert funds from them. God was their provider, as He would be for any new ventures.

And so we went. As is so often with God's callings, it is not because we think we are fit, but we are cornered without escape. They sent us because there was no one else. We had not inspired confidence among the missionaries by my vacillations, and I learned afterwards that they really hadn't confidence in me to rebuild the home end, but it was we or nothing. As Paul says, nothings confound the some-things!

It was a most painful return for us. We ourselves, although we agreed in principle with what *D.C.D.* stood for, knew it could only cause hopeless offence in the homeland; and word getting out about the morphia would finish off everything. And we felt the hurt and sting. We were surely identified with an extremist, but we still said, and we say a thousand times more thirty-five years later, that this was God's extremist, and our greatest honour has been to be allowed to stand with him. But we did not yet know how to see and accept a deep hurt as coming from God, not by permission but by direction, because this is His appointed way. So we were hurt, rather than believed and praised. I remember our feeling when we visited the Keswick Convention that year 1931 and knowing folk around were pointing us out as those who were tarred with that same D.C.D. brush. How comforted we were by one old soldier of the Cross, Frederick Glass, the Bible rough-rider in Latin

America, whom we overheard saying he was glad someone had the courage to stand by the old man.

Because Studd held the veto, however, the Committee (at least those of them who formed the opposition—there were two or three who stood with C.T.) came to recognize that they had no claim to continue the Crusade and no right to dismiss him. So they decided to move out and form a new mission. My brother-in-law, Colonel David Munro, who had married C.T.'s eldest daughter, Grace, one early morning had gone in with me to the mission office next door to the Studd home and removed the address files, etc., to indicate that we were carrying on the work in Studd's name. I think this helped them to see that we were going forward as before, and to leave us to it

It was a close thing. About three weeks later Pauline and I were praying, burdened about the trap we seemed to be in, with more burden than faith. But suddenly, as we prayed, Pauline stopped and said, "Father has gone." And as she said it, I had the confirmation also. Two days later came the cable, and before we opened it we knew what it contained— from Jack Harrison—"Bwana glorified July 16. Hallelujah."

A new era in our lives and in the life of the W.E.C. was about to begin, but as we close the old one, in seeking to describe things as they were, at least as we saw them to be, I hope again one fact stands out above all others—that the great honour of our lives has been to be allowed to be linked with C. T. Studd. Only one other man has had an equal influence on my life. There is no doubt that when all the cards are on the table, there are sides of all our lives which others find difficult to take and wish were different. But the great necessity is to keep the true perspective. We are each as God has created us, and He lives in us as He pleases. Could C.T.S. have been the mighty man of God he was if he had been different in any respects? We don't say this idly because thirty-five years have passed since he went to be with the Lord, and still that life cuts deep furrows for God, where most of his contemporaries are forgotten.

His biography, as I have already said, has changed the lives of thousands by their own admission, and still continues to do so. The mission he founded as this Worldwide Evangelization Crusade never gets away from the standards upon which he founded it—sacrifice, faith and holiness, and never gets away from the constant reminders of what we learned from him. Where one man—called "a museum of diseases" by the doctor—went out, there are over one thousand today in the two Crusades, the W.E.C. and the Christian Literature Crusade; and the other mission which started just before he died, and we can surely claim it as a step-brother, has about five hundred missionaries; and today we have good brotherly fellowship together on the fields and home bases.

We cannot count the tens of thousands, hundreds of thousands, who have heard of Christ through his first step of obedience, in over forty fields. Especially in the Congo are what he could call his greatest joy and crown, among whom his body lies buried—the thousands who have so recently been through their fiery trial and emerged praising God and busy rebuilding their scattered fellowships and greatly adding to their number. And I believe that all this could not have been if Studd had not been the Studd we knew and loved, and still follow in so many ways.

REES HOWELLS—THE SECOND GREAT INFLUENCE ON MY LIFE

As you are able to look back, how plainly you can see God's planning. I was at Keswick in 1928, and two visitors called to see me one afternoon. He was a big man with massive hands and curiously shaped head, with very square forehead and small obtruding ears. His wife was a fairly large and pleasant-looking lady. He said his name was Rees Howells. I had heard that name in reference to some revival in South Africa, but that was all. He said that God had told him to come and see me and to invite me to their Bible College recently started in Swansea, South Wales. I was kind of suspicious and did not respond heartily, but said I would come in September. I really did not intend to go, but when the time came I thought I ought not blatantly to break my word. So I went. I did not realize that this was God forging one of the next great links in the chain of my life.

I am not going to tell the story of Rees Howells in detail because I have had no greater privilege than to put his life story together under the title *Rees Howells Intercessor*. Next to the life of C. T. Studd this has been far the most successful and best selling of the biographies, going so far to eight impressions, some four languages and now in paperback. For me in depth of appeal and understanding of the Lord and His ways, it is my favourite book and I recommend people everywhere to get a copy.

But on my arrival at Glyn Derwen, the first of the four mansions he took by faith for the Bible College and Missionary Children's Home and School, he took me out for a walk in that beautiful area of South Wales. No sooner had he begun to talk than I knew I was listening to the voice of the Spirit through a man, and pure light was streaming into me. The novelty to me was to see the Spirit, not merely as the Indweller but also the Executive of the Trinity in a human body, and directing that person to all kinds of positions of faith and divine love. I had not heard the like before, and one needs to read that book to get the depth of it. I became greatly attached in heart to him, and he privileged me by counting me his special friend.

I paid many visits to him and the college, sat at his feet, drank in from the personal fellowship accompanied by endless hilarity, for it was a job to stop laughing or for him to stop as he described this and that; and then drank in from his tremendous daily meetings with the students, when he would talk for an hour in the morning and another in the evening. What I particularly got from his talks was to see the people of the Old and New Testaments as living persons, not so much to draw detached lessons from them, and still less to see them as some general types, but as living people. He showed them to us going through every kind of pressure and

101

tight corner, and how they believed God, and what is involved in real believing; and then he would line our lives up beside them in our present experiences, illustrating plenty from all he had gone through or was now moving into by faith. He was Welsh, and his English lacked all the polish, with the "h"s all over the place; but here were doctors and college men and women and businessmen eagerly learning the ways of God from this "unlearned" man, and a large company leaving all to join him in his college and world missionary vision.

The importance to me was that I was beginning to catch the principle of faith as God's means of getting things done through us humans, as in Hebrews 11. I made one or two beginner's attempts which fell to the ground, rather like Peter walking on the water and getting a ducking; but he had learned he could walk on water by faith, which the others in the boat had not! Actually it was a right time for experimentation for me. God's time for responsible application had not yet come. The school of faith before the life of faith!

But Mr. Howells was watching W.E.C. developments with me. He had really first contacted me because what he had learned about C. T. Studd made him recognize that here was one of God's marked men of his day, and he wanted to be in touch with what was happening. He said he always knew that a man who made a surrender like C.T. was bound to be used of God, but he would need a successor who had made the same surrender. So when he learned of the schemes and hopes of ousting Studd and capturing and remoulding the mission, he used to laugh and say, "Watch out for God. He will never let His servant down. And you be ready to step in and carry on along these same principles." When the crisis did come, in fact, and we had come home, it was he who said it was a word from the Lord to him that we should boldly go into the offices, remove the records and stake our claim that this was the work God had given C.T., and we were going to carry it on. Mr. Howells turned out right, because I am sure it was that drastic action which made them decide to drop any claims; and only just in time, for in another three weeks there would have been no C. T. Studd and no veto!

I do not mean by this that I could agree with all my friend said and did. Both C.T. and Rees Howells had what I would call the founder temperament. God knows His own business, and, as I have said about C.T., maybe founders have to be largely that type. Both with C.T. and Rees Howells, but with Rees Howells more than C.T., there was a finality about their convictions of what God was saying to them. Rees Howells, once he had said that God had spoken to him about something, would not permit anyone to question it. There was no room for the kind of consultation upon which we have sought God's united guidance in building the modern W.E.C. Yet on the other hand, what God taught him of the ways of the Spirit and did by him, was to me so unique that in some respects I can call myself a disciple of his; and the W.E.C. would by no means be what it is today (unless God did it by some other means), if I had not put into practice what came as such great light to me through him. In his talks he often used to make comparisons between what God did by the men of the Bible, Moses, Elijah and so forth, and what God had done by him, which opened him to the accusations of megalomania by his critics. In addition to this, he made proclamations of faith which in outward appearance failed to materialize and made him seem a false prophet, and he has remained so in the opinion of many.

But I could not see it that way. There is another explanation, which is what I believe, though I'm sure his critics would not. For instance, in his last years, he said he had a thirty-year vision from God which became known as "The Vision" at the Bible College. It was that the world would be evangelized in thirty years, and that they would train at the College a thousand missionaries with whom to do it. Then, when war broke out with Hitler and Mussolini, and it was obvious that under them the world would no longer be free for the spread of the gospel, Rees Howells rose up with an open declaration which he put in print, entitled *God challenges the dictators*, and saying that God would destroy them.

In this he was right, and he had taken a public stand on this in the dark days before even Winston Churchill had done so and in as bold words as any Churchill used. But Rees Howells added to this declaration that the Nazis would be conquered and peace declared by Whitsun 1940. Some national newspapers printed this declaration. Yet on that very day, instead of the destruction of Hitler, his panzer invasion of Holland and Belgium began, followed by Dunkirk and the fall of France. The exact opposite to what Rees Howells had foretold. Yet Mr. Howells still held his praise meeting that Whitsunday in the face of that news.

How could that make sense? It did because from that time onward the company of men and women at the College, about a hundred, as Isaiah said, kept not silence and gave God no rest, until that word of faith became actual substance. That declaration of faith, though mistaken in its date, was to them a point of no return, and without it they would not have done what they did. Night after night through the whole war they battled through in prayer for victory. In his biography the details are given, recorded daily, of the way, probably as no other group in the world at that time, they stood in the gap at critical moments such as at Dunkirk, Alexandria, Stalingrad, Salerno, and gained the victory of faith and declared it beforehand, when nothing but defeat seemed possible. In these ways, though not at that first given date, victory was ultimately complete and the world kept open for the gospel.

Equally in those thirty years, there has been a phenomenal outpouring of missionaries and new missionary organizations, the uprising of the national churches in all countries, and they beginning their own missionary societies, the massive spread of the gospel through radio and literature, which has brought us to the point where we can say that the gospel is being taken to the world—though not directly through the College. Each must read into such incidents what they see; but for myself, I only thank God for men who in the obedience of faith make pronouncements of what God will do and put themselves on the spot by their declarations: and to those who have eyes to see, God does do what they declare He will do, only He does it in His own way. Calvary looked mighty like a failure, and still does so to those without the eye of faith.

I mention these things about my beloved friend above all friends, Rees Howells, as I did about our loved founder C.T., whose place I was destined to take, because it is healthy and balanced to see these other sides of great men, and to prevent us from regarding any man as if he were more than human. I had a difficulty when I wrote both their biographies because of the controversy that was swirling about their heads, and I was with the loyalists who stood with and for them, as I still am. I do not think it would then have been possible, in the coolness and detachment that the distance of a few years now makes, to put this counterbalancing side. Anyhow I did not: but I hope, and say again, that such minor matters are still only seen in perspective. Alfred Buxton put it perfectly in his foreword to C.T.'s life: "Mists that hang about a mountain, but give me the mountain." The defects of virtues, yet God could not get His purposes through such men unless they were just that kind of men.

IV

Living by Faith

LIFE AT W.E.C. LONDON HEADQUARTERS

AND SO WE STARTED AGAIN—IN 1931. THERE WERE ONLY FOUR of us, Pauline and I, Daisy Kingdon from Congo who had stood loyally by Mr. Studd, and Elsie Dexter, the fiancée of one of the Congo missionaries. I don't know how we got the plan of our morning meetings, which really built the new W.E.C. Previously we had a fixed morning half-hour in the office with part Scripture reading and part praying around. We also had an efficient secretary whose philosophy was that if prayer takes a half-hour, business takes eight hours; and she would scrape her chair on the floor as a warning, when the end of the half-hour approached. This was now changed. The important part of the work was now to be to find out without time limits what God is doing in our situations, and then enter into transactions of faith. This is the real business of a mission, and the rest must fit in where it can.

As soon as we started, there came the question, "What are you aiming for?" C.T. had gone, and the mission was in such ill-repute that there had only been £50 that month for the thirty-five workers on the field, so hadn't we better close down? But the next thought was, "What commission did your founder have, which has passed on to you?" We knew that answer—to evangelize the world. "Well, are you going to do it?" "How can we in our present condition and this being the time of world financial depression?" Once again came the thought: "How did the men of the Bible do the impossible?" And, of course, we knew the answer—by faith.

Well, what does faith mean in a practical sense? Somehow we were led to look at Joshua, supposedly because he was in the same tight corner, having just lost his Moses. We saw that God talked with him and told him to go right forward and to be strong and courageous. But then, when that interview had finished, we read—and this is what caught us— that Joshua called together his officers and told them to prepare food, for in three days they would cross that Jordan. But who gave him authority to say that? Then we saw that when we are at God's general disposal to do His will, He puts Himself at our disposal to fill in the details. So it was Joshua who fixed on the three days' limit and God came through with the opening of the Jordan at the time fixed by Joshua.

So we got started. We looked around and said if we were to begin to evangelize the world, we had better begin by immediate reinforcements to Congo. So we fixed on a number—twenty-five reinforcements as a memorial in flesh and blood to C.T., ten by the first anniversary of his glorification, then about nine months ahead, and the other fifteen by the second. God alone was to be trusted both to call the first ten trained and ready to go, and send the money specifically for their outgoing. For all this we put our fingers on Mark 11:24 as a key verse, "Whatsoever ye desire, when ye pray, believe that ye receive them and ye shall have them."

The next day when we met in fellowship again, someone began reminding God about the ten and asking Him to send them. But the Spirit checked us. "If you got them yesterday, why do you ask for them today? Why not be polite and thank?" So we changed our daily asking meetings into thanking, and often laughing, meetings.

One more test came to me next day. It occurred to me that our Congo folks would not have buildings for ten extra ones, and I had better warn them. But wait a minute, supposing they didn't come? I should look a fool, and they would look for another secretary, the same as if Joshua had failed to get that river opened. Of course, the source of that remark was obvious, and I settled it by going myself to the mailbox and putting in the letter.

The actual facts of the progress by faith from then on has been told in the book *After C. T. Studd*, and though out of print now, I will only give a brief outline covering a vast amount of detail, each a drama of faith by itself. That first ten was completed with the last God-called volunteer ten days from the date, and he took with him as his African name Mr. Ten. The last £200 for the finances came two days from the end, while two of us were attending a prayer conference in Ireland and were watching for the miracle as the days lessened—five, four, three, two; and then a telegram from Pauline from London to say "£200 for the ten. Hallelujah." The thrill of this was not so much the completion of the ten as the confirmation that we were on the main line of the Bible principles of faith.

After the ten, there were the fifteen the next year, completed within two weeks of the date; the next year twenty-five; the next year fifty; the next year seventy-five. We then stopped taking these annual quotas, as we were expanding to a number of new fields and could not get the workers out as quickly as they were coming in.

I should add that, if you looked closely into details, there was usually some small spot where the supply was not exactly as we had asked for it, though that was not so in the ten and fifteen; but we used to crack a joke and say in such launches of faith, if we got 90 per cent, we were thankful enough.

By this time others among us had begun to see this was the key to the practice of Scriptural faith—that where we are in the calling of God, as we are at His disposal, so He is at ours; we can "ask what we will", and believe that we receive what we have asked. Fields began to be opened by this means.

Pat Symes went to Colombia pinpointing the town in which he would start amidst all the fanatical opposition in those early years, and declaring that God would send fifty workers in ten years. They came, though, as in all fields, there were battles and difficulties and many left. But who could believe that barren and difficult field is the Colombia of today with the Training Centre crowded with students, with many churches and all in the hands of national leadership, and new response and congregations springing up all around?

111

We put up a map of West Africa with arrows pointing to seven fields needing evangelization, and spoke the word of faith for the experienced leader as a start, and then for the occupation of all the seven. Sam Staniford of long experience in the Congo had returned with double cataract; but instead of going back to home teaching, responded to God's call to take the lead. He opened the work in the Ivory Coast, and entry followed into Senegal, Liberia, Ghana, Portuguese Guinea (by a woman alone when three men, who first went in, left again—Bessie Fricker, now Brierley; and this gave us one of our W.E.C. mottoes, "The woman is the man to do it"!). All those fields have their missionary workers today with churches and evangelists. Alec Thorne went to Spanish Guinea by a deliberate act of faith when the Spanish Government would not give a visa. When he landed, instead of being turned out, he found the Governor to be one who had been impressed with Protestant missionary work in another country, and so let him in and advised him where to start. The Okak tribe today has its twenty and more churches, with its own national leaders and evangelists. The seventh field to which we had directed an arrow of faith has been entered by another mission.

India and Pakistan; Borneo, Sumatra, Java; Brazil and Uruguay; Japan, Thailand, Korea; Canary Islands, Dominica, Formosa, Chad, Sardinia, Trucial States, Gambia, Venezuela, Upper Volta, Vietnam, Iran have all followed. But a list of names will only weary readers, except to give a glimpse into the outburst of the Spirit, on a world-wide scale, which has completely confirmed that first apparently wild statement that C.T. made when he left for the heart of Africa alone in 1913. Thought to be crazy, leaving his wife an invalid, penniless except for the supply of his fare, himself warned that he would die, we have told how he wrote back from board ship, "God has spoken to me in strange fashion and said, This trip is not just for the heart of Africa, but for the whole unevangelized world. To human reason it sounds ridiculous, but faith laughs at impossibilities and cries it shall be done": and how he had coupled it with the motto which he wrote on a postcard the night before sailing: "If Jesus Christ be God and died for me, then no sacrifice can be too great for me to make for Him."

How right he had also been in encountering the criticisms of the committee that he had lost his world-wide vision by saying, "God sent me to Congo and on Congo I centre my attention; but God will raise up others, just as He called me, for these other lands." And so it was. And it was by this principle of faith. C.T. lived faith; but from Rees Howells I learned how to operate faith as the principle of God's action by man. This was to be God's way, hidden from C.T. during his lifetime, by which His word to him would be fulfilled. Each of those fields could fill pages with their stories of God's moving in by faith and doing the impossible. "The people that do know their God shall be strong and do exploits." And these have been exploits of faith.

FAITH WORKS AT HOME

Naturally I have been in touch with the various home-base developments, where we have been seeing years of miracles, and far beyond just the first British base. A revolutionary step which has greatly affected all that has followed was when Pauline and I were led to take one further position of faith. I believe it remains unique among missionary societies, and has always subjected us to criticism, as being ridiculous and fanatical; but we would not change it after thirty-five years, not one of us; its values in so many ways are so great and widespread among us. I don't know whether I picked it up from Rees Howells' Bible College where they live by the same principle; probably I did. But after C.T.'s death, when things were so tight and apparently shaky, Pauline and I decided that, with so little money to send to the field and we ourselves in the security and comforts of the homeland, the least sacrifice we could make would be to take nothing from mission funds for ourselves and our three children, but live by Jesus' word in Matthew 6:33, "Seek ye first the kingdom of God and his righteousness, and all these things shall be added unto you."

But we were very soon in the need of help. Grace Walder had been an assistant secretary in the work with a regular salary, but less than she might have earned in other employment. She had remained with us on the same terms as before, and I do not know how we should have picked up the threads of the work without her. She has been with us until her retirement last year, together with her assistant, Peggy Chapman, somehow managing to take on more and more of the business end of things as the work has so greatly grown.

I needed someone to help in my correspondence, and someone to represent the work round the country who had himself had Congo experience. What hope could there be of co-workers who would join us with no salary or allowance, nothing beyond what God sent them personally for their personal needs? So here was another opportunity for speaking the word of faith. We did so. It seems a little thing now, when it has become common for others to join us on these conditions. But when none had ever done it, so far as we knew, in a missionary society, it was a different matter.

I don't know how Elizabeth Hand, a middle-aged lady, heard of us or our need, except that she belonged to a remarkable little mission hall in Acton, West London, from which twenty-four have gone into full-time service (fifteen into W.E.C.) out of a membership of about sixty! Among these have been several of our leading Weccers including Len and Percy Moules, and of the Smith family Charlton, Eric, Olive and Iris. But Elizabeth came and offered, and joined us to do my letters. "Ma Hand", we used to call her in the African fashion.

Alfred Ruscoe had been with us in Congo. He had left as a critic of C.T., but had learned his lesson by going to another mission field where he found what it was to be under a real dictator in the flesh. After returning home, in his spiritual need he was caught hold of at a convention by Mrs. Rees Howells, went down to be with them, and had a tremendous personal experience of the Holy Ghost taking over in place of the self-life. Finding also that Rees Howells was such an admirer of C.T. and understood the depths of C.T.'s walk of faith and obedience as God's intercessor, he saw how shallow and foolish his critical attitudes had been. For a time he joined the Friends Evangelistic Band, where he learned to renew his faith life for personal needs and found such joy in it that he never wanted to go back again to the human security level.

At this juncture I knew none of all this. I had gone to Liverpool to speak at a Memorial Meeting for C.T. I was used to critics in my audiences; but there was *the* critic under my nose in the front row—Alfred Ruscoe with whom I had always had a deep spiritual affinity, but from whom I had parted. That cost me my liberty when I began to speak with him present! But I got over it. At the end, up came Alfred for a handshake, and of all things, clean against my normal instincts, I said to him, "Why don't you come and join us again?" It shocked him as much as me. But we both recognized the voice of God. However, we arranged to meet again, and meanwhile I felt sure I should escape my ill-advised invitation because he would surely want an allowance. We met, and the first thing Alfred said was, "Yes, I'll come under one condition. I will take no allowance, I am relearning the adventure of trusting God!" Here were the two of them—Alfred and Elizabeth.

But as with The Ten, it was not just these two, but the discovery of a new way in which we could trust God in a faith mission. God could call for the home-base those who would trust Him for personal needs and leave the mission funds for the fields, and thus be linked with the field-workers in that much of sacrifice.

Of course, I had no idea how a few snowflakes were going to become an avalanche. Here we are thirty-six years later, with home-bases in many lands and with all the home-base workers living on these same principles, single workers, couples, families, and all daily proving the Lord's faithfulness.

To think of the personal blessing that has been mine since Ma Hand was the first to join me! She married after a few years, and soon after went to the Lord through cancer. Then for all my years in England, from 1937 until we came to the U.S.A. in 1957, Fred Anthony was my intimate co-worker, I can only say serving me as he has served Christ. When I came to the U.S.A., Anne Easley joined me for several years until she went south to care for her mother; and finally right up to the present, Mildred McCadden has been with me, day after day at the typewriter.

Can anyone imagine a more wonderful service of love to God than I have enjoyed through all these years? How many millions of words have they typed! And God alone their provider. We have worked on a fellowship basis. I have never had a secretary, only co-workers. We share the mail, discuss the problems, and, rather than dictate to shorthand, I have always dictated straight to the typewriter, so that we could stop and make a correction or discuss a point. So it has been real co-working. But that does not mean I have been easy to work with. I know I have strong convictions and am often argumentative. Also being quick in temperament, I am fussy about minor points which slow things up; and I think my co-workers are marvels of patience. They have the grace of stickability. But though I often fail in grace and patience in daily details, I can say that I always hold them in honour and speak of them to others in terms of the glory of Christ in their lives; for they are "the glory of Christ" (2 Cor. 8:23), and in their hidden way do not "regard their lives" in the service of Christ (Phil. 2:29, 30).

Gradually, the home departments of the work developed on these faith lines. The kitchens, the offices, the household work, the deputation department, the magazine and printing departments, the practical work in the gardens, in repairs and painting, the car maintenance: the workers for all these God sending and settling in through the years in their hidden background ministries, and all for the Lord without human remuneration. Most people who hear of it don't believe it—

but it is a fact! The overheads are met by mission funds—heating and lighting, and office expenses—but nothing personal.

DAILY GUIDANCE AND FAITH SESSIONS

The London Headquarters started with C.T.'s personal home, a twelve-roomed four-storey brick house, No. 17 Highland Road, Upper Norwood. From this one house we gradually expanded. A cats' and dogs' home next door was taken for the offices. A hostel was built by faith with our own work team, which included the erection of steel girders (which incidentally kept it intact through the bombing), under the supervision of our W.E.C. friend, Uncle Hoppy (Will Hopkins) and his nephew Wilfrid Watt, a building contractor. The money was sent specifically for that purpose, and it was designed with a communal dining-room into which we could pack seventy-five for the crowded monthly conferences, and bedrooms for sixteen. Other surrounding houses were bought cheaply in the same road after they had been shaken and evacuated through the London bombing, until we had reached an average community, with our C.L.C. co-workers, of seventy—home-base workers, furlough missionaries and candidates, in Nos. 17, 19, 19A, 32, 34 and 2 Highland Road, No. 9 Hawke Road and No. 5 Harold Road.

Morning by morning we had our fellowship meetings—of course, much enlarged now—and I took them as my personal commission when at home. Nothing was formal. We sat in a circle, no special leader in a special place of prominence. We sang a song or two; John Whittle had prepared a special book of about sixty songs of the type that suited us, not the softening, comforting ones of all woe till we get to heaven's peace, but such as: "When mountain walls confront thy way, Why sit and weep? Arise and say, Be thou removed, and they shall be, By power of God cast in the sea"; "The walls of Jericho were strong, But stronger was the Mighty Lord . . ."; "Give me the love that leads the way, The faith that nothing will

117

dismay . . . Let me not sink to be a clod, Make me thy fuel, Flame of God." Then a free time of worship and prayer and personal sharing of what God is doing in our daily lives. Then we get down together to immediate challenges on fields or home bases or to new fields, always with freedom for the give and take of discussion, encouraging the youngest to participate. We head up in the critical question, "What is God saying to us now which requires the decision and declaration of faith?" Sometimes it would be several days before we would have a united assurance that this or that was God's mind. Then Scripture and a talk over some incident, often from the lives of the men of faith, by which we could learn how to believe.

Actually it was these morning meetings which forced me to find living material from the Bible. I never had Bible training and have never taught consecutively. Now I was compelled morning by morning to share something relevant. They laugh now at the blank spaces in early days when I didn't know what to say next. But they became great times, especially as we lived again with Moses, Abraham, Joshua, David, Elijah and the rest of them. They really spoke to us. I have no difficulty now in finding the Book speaking to me wherever I open it. So I say to folk that the best way to find the Bible coming alive to you is to be forced to give it to others. I have never used commentaries, or very rarely. I have always felt it was better that I should get what was original to me, even if thin material.

In these meetings, we began to see the need of home-base extensions, both in Britain and overseas. So we pinpointed and took by faith a series of regional Headquarters, the necessary houses and personnel, which could become living fellowship and faith centres in various areas of Britain, and for spreading the challenge of world evangelization and enlisting of recruits. We put a map of faith in the magazine, drawn, as was all our art work, by our Charlton Smith. He had given up an art career in wallpaper designing with its comfortable income to join with us and become one of my earliest intimates; and he has never been afraid to tell me where I was getting off! The map listed twelve prospective centres. These have never all been occupied, but a good many have: Glasgow, Belfast, Swansea, Bristol, Leeds, Birmingham, Southampton. The staff for each, some couples and some single women, heard the call, and the provision of a house in each city has been equally a gift from God with no mission funds used. Each has carried on its work, taking no funds from the mission either for personal needs or overheads. They prepare tours for missionary teams in contact with churches in their area. They visit the groups, which we call prayer batteries, who meet in homes and use the information they get from the fields for prayer. They use their regional headquarters for fellowship with many who come to get spiritual refreshment. Part of my job was to visit my co-workers in these headquarters and keep them up to date with our problems and encouragements, and share theirs with them.

But what has seemed to us a series of miracles through the years, in the London Headquarters, in obtaining all these houses close together, in the growth of the faith staff, in the preservation through the bombing with buzz-bombs falling next door, and in the regional headquarters, has now been capped by what seems like a miracle of miracles. Three years ago, the London County Council announced that they were clearing us all out to build a series of high rise apartments. Len Moules, who has now taken my place as International Secretary, and Iris his wife, were in charge. They had told them they would give us market value compensation for our houses, which would not be so great considering their age. This would never have done for us because we did not need just some scattered houses we could buy here and there; we are a community and needed resettlement as a community. We had a Christian lawyer representing us, and I don't know how it happened, but the County Council admitted the validity of our claim to be re-established as a community, and stated that they would compensate us if we could find suitable accommodation.

119

After an extensive search, the right place was found, a beautiful estate of 70 acres in the Green Belt with a main building of 115 rooms besides other houses, being offered for sale by a religious group—Bulstrode, at Gerrard's Cross, not far from Windsor. The County Council bought it for us with another generous amount for removal, repairs and restoration. This has been a tremendous provision of God for us, far outweighing our former separate houses. Here we are able to bring together various scattered activities, such as the Youth Centre from Birmingham, and the Printery from Scotland, with plenty of room for a conference centre, youth camps, foreign student work and a welcome for guests and visitors, particularly for the many W.E.C. friends who give us so much hospitality about the country. I had been responsible for the buying of our former homes, and though I cannot give accurate figures, we bought them cheaply, and the sum of money which the County Council has given us for our new home is about twelve times the amount we paid for them. A thousand friends gathered for the opening conference, Easter 1968. Even allowing for the rise in prices, it does seem that the Lord worked a miracle for us just when money is so tight in Britain.

LEADERSHIP BY STAFF FELLOWSHIP

The depth of the fellowship we have had these years in the W.E.C. is a result of the second innovation upon which we restarted the work; and we are as sure today that it was of God as we were then. Again I don't know how it became clear to me as the right principle for our developments. Two of the former committee members had remained with us, but they soon recognized that the change in our future form of Mission government made the existence of an Executive Committee unnecessary, so we dissolved ourselves. C.T. had left a letter appointing me as President of W.E.C. in place of himself; but I saw quite clearly that a founder may have certain rights of veto which his successor should not claim, and that it was sufficient for a successor just to be secretary. Also I was very clear—and I believe it to be the New Testament principle—that a functioning fellowship of God's people, be they a church or society, should manage their own affairs without outside control; and that this was the only basis of total fellowship, when all who have given themselves to a work have the same rights of unitedly exploring and discussing and deciding on their courses of action. The division between managers and managed is deadly and death to total heart fellowship in freedom, unless the managers and managed are merely members of the managed, voluntarily chosen for management, and with open opportunities for all concerned to thrash things out together.

So we began the system in which all full-time W.E.C. workers at the home-base or on furlough from the fields form the executive staff for the affairs of that home-base. We met weekly one evening and came to any necessary immediate decisions. As we expanded, in order to give the chance for our regional co-workers or missionaries on furlough to be with us, we had quarterly meetings lasting for two or three days. The length of time gave us plenty of opportunity unhurriedly to seek God's mind, which is impossible if the Committee consists of a few busy people who can only meet for an hour or so. It also meant that our staff meetings could be for times of spiritual refreshment with the first hours given to unhurried prayer, sharing and fellowshipping around the Word. The fact that all full-timers could be part of this executive staff gave the newest comers the sense from the beginning that they were the W.E.C. and not some employees of the W.E.C.

Often such staff meetings need patience, because there is room and time for free discussion; and the task of the "chairman", the field or home-base leader, is not to impose some idea of his own, but to catch the tone of the meeting and voice what obviously seems to be the mind of God coming through. No votes are taken, because votes divide. Like the Quakers of old, the "sense of the meeting" is sought.

We knew secretaries of other missions who said it was ridiculous to think a missionary society could be run on such lines; and what was worse in those earlier days we never even kept "minutes" or had "agenda". But it has just not been so; and with the great increase of the W.E.C. into so many fields and home-bases, there is no desire on the part of any to change. Indeed, the other way round, for all feel heart satisfied that by this means we are all and each "The W.E.C."; and we so often note that when any have left us, they still have those nostalgic feelings of being part of us and that W.E.C. is their real home.

I suppose this system might not be workable at a home-base where all are not on the same unsalaried basis, where some may be employed who are sincere servants of Christ, but who have not responded to or even had a call to total identification with the society. But where none are on the staff who have not had a personal call from God to give themselves to be in the Crusade full-time and for life, and where there are no variable levels of salary, then it is easy for all to be part of the executive staff. The effect for the missionary candidate is the same. They come to live with us at the Headquarters of their homeland for a period of at least six months, soaking in the projects of faith and the Crusade principles at the morning meetings, and thoroughly getting to know us and we them. So they do not find themselves just "accepted" by a Board they don't know, but given the right hand of fellowship into a company who for life and death are the called together of God for world evangelization.

It is this that always made my visits about the country to our regional headquarters as from W.E.C. home to W.E.C. homes; and it has been the same in going to homes and families who began to catch the sense that they too were part of this W.E.C. fellowship, and who used their homes to welcome Weccers and forward the work. They were just family gatherings and sharings of all that was going on, bad or good, and entering into local problems, with no hold-backs; for there were no secrets within the family, and no sense of superiority as if some big or important visitor had come.

I do not mean by this that I have ever found fellowship easy, cheap or automatic. I am naturally at heart a loner and don't want to meet people. Maybe way back there is some inferiority complex that is responsible for this. But when a person comes to see me, unless it is one I am already at home with, I wish they wouldn't! So foolish, because as soon as I am with them, I am glad they have come, and coldness changes to warm interest. I am also intensely critical. For years I have had a battle there, and though in general by now the critical attitude is overflowed by acceptance and appreciation, the critical tiger can quickly show his claws. This is mostly so with those with whom I am closest. I am so quickly conscious of what irks me about them (and it is ghastly to think how much must irk them about me); and I am conscious that it often tinges my spirit and attitude towards them in the small contacts of life. I had that for long towards Pauline, and I will tell later when and how a real change came. Towards my children also I am so quick to see where I think they fall short, instead of seeing by faith that God is at work on them as He was on me; and no one could have been a nastier little boy and more conceited teenage lad than I. I have not let these minor daily rubs break connections with people or blow up into storms; but they have rather been niggling reactions, which remain niggling and minor, while I seek to maintain in general the larger sense of constant thankfulness for such co-workers, for Christ so evident in them, and constant appreciation of their lives outpoured for the Lord.

But in a Crusade fellowship as large as we have become, we are never without rifts between one another appearing on the surface. We just have to face it as part of brotherhood in Christ! My forty-nine years give me full proof of that. We have never been without some personal battles going on somewhere. I have been mixed in my share of them. Not one of our fields is without gaps from those who have come and gone, sometimes in large numbers, over a period of years. Perhaps quite naturally it often shocks newcomers when they find this; and they think that relationships or leadership or something on this or that field must be pretty shaky. No—just the usual thing! And the worst of all were those early Congo years. Yet Christ continues to found His church on the rock of Himself working through His Peters, and the gates of hell can't prevail against them.

The answer, we know, is to see Christ in our brother, and accept his humanity, even as Christ has accepted him; and on the whole we do this: and if there are the gaps where there have been casualties, there are the solid ranks of the soldiers shoulder to shoulder; and we are far more conscious of the bonds of our world-wide fellowship, and happy in it, than we are of the breaks here or there.

Fellowship is the fourth pillar of W.E.C.—sacrifice, faith, holiness, fellowship. This last has really been added in this W.E.C. generation. The wounds of those early years, and the losses, left a scar in me, which God has turned to good—because I took up my responsibilities in 1931 with one great determination—that we should not break in pieces again. This has been so by God's enablings.

I believe we can all bear witness that the fellowship in W.E.C. world-wide fields and home-bases, is real and healthy, loving and honest, and that the fourth pillar is a pillar among us. In a fine leaf-covered tree, if you look closely, you can see leaves with holes on them where the caterpillars have had a feed, but stand back and you are thrilled with its leafy luxuriance.

THE ENCOURAGEMENT OF INDIVIDUAL INITIATIVE

In building the work on the fellowship principle, I always had it in mind that there should be room for individual initiative. So often Boards with their cautious approach, or even staff fellowships by too much use of fellowship authority, can choke the originality of the Spirit. I have always been keen to preserve that freedom in W.E.C. which would permit individual experiment, even when the rest of us can't see the wisdom of it. After all, W.E.C. was born like that. We had a founder who started out after his committee had dissolved themselves because they could not support him!

One such of great significance for W.E.C. developments was the start of our Training Centre in Glasgow. A business couple had sold their store to go to Colombia. They then went through a "wilderness" patch, in which everything seemed to go wrong, and they landed back in England apparently on the shelf and by-passed by God for whom they had sold all—God's usual training and testing methods! They reluctantly agreed to take on what was already the small beginning of a Scottish headquarters; but as they became more and more stirred by the young people who gathered round them, almost surreptitiously and certainly not with my backing, they began to develop a training centre. When it was sufficiently going for us not to be able easily to stop it they presented it to us to be the W.E.C. M.T.C. (Missionary Training College it is called, though I prefer Centre or Colony, because it is out to produce missionary trainees, not college students). What could we do but say, "The Lord be with you"? and we knew He was.

If anyone wants to read in a few pages how something can be built, expanded, sustained, how one can give an adequate training, send out dozens of missionaries, on not a thing but the faithfulness of God and the most daring acts of faith for large sums in the tightest corners—the most unique faith-testimony in our history—get Fran and Elsie Rowbotham's little brochure, *Would you believe it?* To this was added, by the generous gift of our friend Austin Sparks—a gift when he might well have asked a price for it—the mansion and grounds of Kilcreggan House, near the Isle of Bute, which the Rowbothams have developed into a conference centre crowded all the summer.

From this came the inspiration to start a Training Centre for Australia and New Zealand on the island of Tasmania, to which went Stewart and Marie Dinnen, who had been principals in the Glasgow Centre, and which is now equally expanding and crowded with trainees; and now another is starting in Durban, South Africa.

The greatest unheralded outbirth of W.E.C. has been the Christian Literature Crusade. I was involved in the scheme to slip it into existence without giving the staff or other home-bases the chance to approve or to clamp down on it. The reason for this was that, though we knew it was of God, a straight literature crusade would be considered a little out of line with W.E.C.'s direct commission; and we were taking no chances. It started, like so many of God's works, almost incidentally and almost out of a joke. In war days when shops could not be opened or literature obtained, Kenneth and Bessie Adams approached us with a view to representing W.E.C. in the east of England. But when we talked with them, they already had a little upstairs bookstore in the small town of Colchester, and they laid down one condition—they must continue the store. That was the kind of ultimatum which, if we had a hide-bound outlook, we should have to refuse. How carry on an itinerant deputation ministry and be tied to a small bookstore? But already some among us had been challenging us to do more in literature, so I was pre-pared ground. When, therefore, they made this condition, with this need of literature in mind, it came like a flash and almost like a joke to say, "All right, let's start a kind of Christian Literature Woolworths, with stores all round this country and the world." So it was settled, and the C.L.C. was born.

It has been some healthy baby, now grown to independent manhood, twenty-seven years old. The staff, when they heard, did raise many questions, and my cautious Pauline was among them. But it was too late—consent or no consent! I worked very closely with Ken, and the others who soon joined him, the Whybrows, Booths, Charlton Smiths, Fittons, Dorrie Brooking and others. We hammered out a constitution which would from the first give them total autonomy, handling their own business, finance and developments, though on the same total faith basis, with home-workers unsalaried, as in W.E.C. We joined as one in our staff meetings, and all candidates were tested and accepted in our combined commissions. I always saw and said that if C.L.C. was of God, as I was sure it was, it should grow much bigger than its parent W.E.C., though I often annoyed Weccers by saying this. But it is obviously so, because W.E.C. takes the Gospel to specific fields of its own, thanking God for other missions who go to other areas. But C.L.C. is a church-wide, mission-wide, world-wide ministry to bring books that point to Christ to all lands and all churches in all lands.

It has its own thrilling story to tell, which they gave me the privilege of writing in book form in *The Leap of Faith*; and here it is spreading round the world, with headquarters in Britain, the U.S.A. and Australia, and with literature centres in thirty countries with ninety bookstores and fifty book-mobiles, a staff of over three hundred, and a book distribution well over six figures in dollars annually. There have been tensions. I have always had perfect fellowship and understanding with Ken Adams and the other leaders; and in the earlier days we always met weekly and monthly as one staff. As the two Crusades expanded to other home-bases, there were questions of interrelationship which had to be ironed out, and sometimes there was disharmony.

Now that the C.L.C. has "come of age", the two Crusades are organizationally separate, but there remain the close family bonds (very many of the CLCers started as WECers), through which there is interchanging of workers and inter-mingling on fields, and in staff and in public, and the sharing of accommodations. Nothing thrills me more than that God should have used W.E.C. to be flexible enough to produce C.L.C. and nurture it in its younger days.

I have noticed also how, if we give God room enough, He can take square pegs out of round holes and put them in the square holes where they fit. One of our most fruitful later activities, which I have not had much directly to do with, but did with the workers in their round hole days, are the Gospel broadsheets we call *Soon* in the English edition, *Bientôt* in the French and *Cedo* in the Portuguese. They are large single sheets, with printed matter on both sides, in simple English, French and Portuguese, which can be read by the large numbers of almost every country of the world today who know one or other of these languages and can read them if in simple form. They mainly contain witnesses from nationals or news which can get attention on the world situation especially oriented to the Lord's Coming, which is why the title is *Soon*. They are sent out in hundreds of thousands for distribution, not merely among churches and mission folk but also to officials, clerks, business folk not normally reached. A great many letters come back from those who find Christ and want more.

Bientôt, the first, was started by Fred Chapman and his French wife, Lois. Fred had a true missionary heart, had worked in the Ivory Coast and Congo, but was not an easy fitter-in, a loner maybe, but one of those whose jaws you cannot get open again once his teeth are in a thing. I always knew Fred's worth and stuck by him and fought for him. Now he needs no man to fight for him. By some flash of inspiration, he started *Bientôt*, and its success was immediate and enormous. They were given a house as *Bientôt* headquarters in Worthing, and gathered their own volunteer working staff around them, and now there's no stopping them.

John Lewis was another. He was the third with Fred Anthony, with whom I worked closely for many years at London Headquarters, we three opening and discussing the mail daily together. But I always knew there was something restless about John. He had a probing, organizing mind, penetrating into and inquiring into everything. He was a good disagreer, though that does not make for easy relationships! But his potential was obvious. For a time he organized our deputation department and his ability was plain enough in that. But he was not happy. He had not found his feet and knew it, and so did others around him. Then

128

Above: *With the family—Priscilla, Paul and Daniel—in 1942*

Below: *The W.E.C. Co-ordinating Council, 1964. l. to r.: Dave Cornell, Ivor Davies, Norman Grubb, Len Moules, David Batchelor, Arthur Davidson*

Pauline

Norman

Getting on in years!

came the flash to him. Start an English *Bientôt—Soon*. His whole heart went into this. He and his wife, Eleanor (Nellie), were given on what appears to be a permanent loan, a lovely house some miles out of London. The demands and open doors for an English *Soon* were even greater than *Bientôt*! They are immersed in the outpouring of tens of thousands, with his staff of workers living with them, and a hundred or two of *Soon* Service Clubs about the country who take responsibility for sending out the packages.

Neither of these thriving ministries, and obviously costing plenty, receive any mission funds, but are built and expanded on what God sends by faith. I am thankful that my little part in this, very little, was to keep tight hold in fellowship and expectancy on these two, till the pegs have fitted tightly into their holes. I think W.E.C. has to beware. I know of others, individualists, men with elbows which get into ribs, but marked men of God; but we lose them because we cannot stretch our fellowship wide enough to be tolerant of them, see the potential greatness and hold on.

Phil Booth is another, and Miriam his wife, though not so peggish but somehow with his obvious brilliance and ability not fitting fully in. He made a sacrifice as a business executive while still young, and threw up plenty of worldly prospects to join W.E.C. and C.L.C. There were times when the question arose—at least in my mind—was he for leadership in either W.E.C. or C.L.C.? And on one occasion I proposed him. But no. Perhaps his mind was too brilliant, and W.E.C. is not much used to brilliance of that kind, and he would say things in ways a little different from and beyond the ordinary. I don't know. Anyhow, by God's grace he stuck by us, as we by him. Then came his open door—Radio Worldwide, producing tapes for many distant and scattered radio stations which bring the message of Christ, yet in unusual forms, such as "Books for Banishment", "They came to Britain", "It's all yours"—and that brilliance has found its niche and usefulness. He studied and made himself expert on his subject.

Nine others have joined them who are trained for this work. They occupy one of W.E.C.'s larger houses which is not being taken by the County Council; and it is amazing to see how they have fixed up the top floor to contain all the (to an amateur) intricate instruments for his tape preparations. The accommodation—still unprofessional (until the Lord gives the housing sought for), but not the productions. Phil is a founder member of the Evangelical Radio Alliance in Britain. And once again, all by God's provision, outside of W.E.C. funds.

Charlie and Lily Searle had their frustrations, not in personality but in health. They seemed finished after a long tour in Congo, owing to Lily's heart condition. They were out of the mission for a time, and then back with Charlie doing deputation work, and Lily with their five children telling Charlie to go ahead. He must not be concerned for them; God would be their provider. Lily has told her story in *Going through with God*. But that kind of going through —with God—has God's surprises at the other end. Unexpected, rarely successful, though greatly rewarding, and taking all of God's love and wisdom. It has been the bringing up for their parents and for God the children the missionaries entrusted to them. I was involved with them in this, when one day together we spoke the word of faith that at the finish of World War II God would give a place with the exact specifications we outlined to Him—the most definite and detailed we ever asked of Him; a large house, with sufficient grounds for the children to play in; with a surrounding wall to keep them from the highway; near enough for primary, secondary schooling and ultimately college; and with as good a climate as Britain can provide for children from the Tropics. The story of how that came exactly according to specifications, and with the sum of money with which to buy it, the mansion in Scotland, the grounds surrounded with the wall, the furnishings and educational facilities, has been told in Charlie Searle's little booklet, *Can God*.

But way beyond this in importance was the wisdom and

130

grace given these two and their helpers to be parents through the years to about sixty of our children, making a real home for them with right disciplines, yet with children's fun and interests, sound development, good education, but always remaining the children of their parents. Nearly all these, now young men and women, left the home knowing the Lord, and many serving Him. The whole family all these years were fed directly from the hand of the Lord, the mission only paying the house overheads, heating, etc.

These were my team-mates from 1931 to 1957 when Pauline and I came to the U.S.A. I have, of course, only mentioned a few. God's family is a wonderful family even on earth. If Paul could boast of his redeemed family, can not I? We were and are bound together in love, and I hold them in highest admiration: Jock Purves, my closest associate, the one among us who always pointed us to brotherly love; for some years Leslie Sutton, my beloved friend from Cambridge days; Bill and Ena Pethybridge who founded our youth work, and with whom I was always so close in spirit; Charlton Smith, our W.E.C. artist and gifted speaker. The faithful ones in those regional headquarters without the intimacy of fellowship and interchange of information we could have in London: Willie Weir in Belfast; Matsya Howard, Alice Barnes, Phyllis Gallup in Bristol; Kathleen Hammond and Nellie Marsh in Southampton; Kay Duddridge in Birmingham; Jessie Scott and Iris Davies in Swansea; Albert and Hilda Burrows in Leeds; Wesley Cunningham in Glasgow; Ken and Mavis Gabriel in the youth work. I feel I must at least mention these, though it still leaves some unmentioned. My list of Romans, chapter 16!

And along with these are the close friendships of years which have bound us as one family with so many around the country; their homes have been my homes, and we have shared our mutual interests and burdens. They have been as much a part of W.E.C. as any of us, and their sacrifices for Christ and the work have been just as real. I suggested the name of "over-timers" for them some years back, and it has stuck. Our missionary job is our full-time job; theirs is over-time after they have done their day's work.

There were a few who were specially dear to me who stood with us through the stormy days of 1931 and were not moved by rumours flying around; and then there are others who came into the family later: John and Lena Govan of Belfast (John is now with the Lord); Sidney and Muriel Brown of Manchester (Sidney now with the Lord); Ben and Mary Woodall (near Manchester); Elsie Rowan and Florence Allan and Kathleen Wright of Nottingham; Hollie Welch and J. C. Young of Newcastle; Stanley and Jessie Oglesby of York (Stanley now with the Lord), and their daughter Margaret, and Jim Fields and Douglas Greenfield also of York; Gwen Watkins of Bristol; Jack and Alice Yates of Birmingham; Ted and Ethel Bushell of Liverpool; Isa Moore (now in the U.S.A.), her sisters and the unique Tommy Stockman of Ballymena; Eva and Clara Stuart Watt of Dublin (Eva with the Lord); Cyril and Daisy Hood of Sheffield (Cyril with the Lord); John and Nellie Stewart (now in the U.S.A.), and Willie and Barbara Johnston of Glasgow; Phyllis Brown of Brighton; Anne Rees (now Robinson) and her late father of Richmond; Rona Bradley of Haywards Heath; Captain Lang of Lingfield; Mair Lewis and Kathleen Hancox (now McGrath) formerly of London H.Q.; Laura Guest (who with her husband, now with the Lord, were Regional H.Q. workers) of Bournemouth; Joyce Haime and her sisters of Bideford; Maynard James and Jack Ford now leading lights in the British Nazarenes; Dr. Priddy, Miss Ruscoe, Dr. Symonds, Miss Williams and so many others of the staff of the Bible College of Wales. Most readers can skip this list, but I could not pass them by.

V

Adventures in Faith

THE MENTION OF ALL THESE FAITH DEVELOPMENTS MIGHT GIVE the idea that all is sunny in the faith life, and the land always flowing with milk and honey. But by no means so. It would probably be a shock and surprise if we had a list of all the hundreds of times the pockets of all of us were absolutely empty. And why not? Paul's standard was that Christ should be magnified in him whether by life or by death; and he knew how to be abased as well as to abound.

One of my favourite Scriptures which I have used among us dozens of times, was when Paul warned the Corinthian church about the danger of thinking themselves to be well off because they were full and rich, "and reigned as kings without us"; but God's standard for apostleship (and I reckon the called of God are the apostles) is "appointed to death . . . spectacles to the world . . . fools . . . weak . . . despised; hungry, thirsty, naked, buffeted, with no certain dwelling place: labouring with our own hands, reviled, persecuted, defamed, and as the filth of the world and offscouring of all things" (1 Cor. 4:9–13). That has always kept us from thinking that we approached within a hundred miles of apostolic and Scriptural standards of the missionary calling; and that if we have appeared a little more extreme than some, we are miles from the extremes of our forerunners. So personal financial shortage is a very little thing. Paul's standard again suits us: "having food and raiment, let us therewith be content".

We are not saying that God calls others to go this way, and we are thankful, as Paul was, for those who have this world's goods and the comforts of life, and who so freely use them for God. Paul did not tell the rich to give away their riches; but, while warning them of special dangers and snares in wealth, told them to "do good, be rich in good works, ready to distribute, willing to communicate". And where would all of us be who have this special calling of serving Christ, if there were not the Gaius's whom John thanks for his well-known "charity to the brethren and to strangers"? So I thank God for those who have this world's goods, and whose ministry in the Gospel is at least partly by the distribution of them.

We had our tight times specially in our earlier days, when we were just starting to live as a household by faith. We were then about ten in the house. We also had with us C.T.'s mother's old personal maid, from the days when the Studd family lived in Hyde Park Gardens off Park Lane (these are the years described by Edith, C.T.'s daughter, in her new book already referred to on page 66). Now retired, the old lady had her home with us, though out of kindness she insisted on cooking for the household. Miss Musset by name, called "Muss" by all of us, she professed to laugh at our weird ideas of living on the promises of God, though she liked the young candidates, especially the boys, whom she called "the Hallelujah Boys". She lived in the basement where we had our dining-room and kitchen, but would not eat with us. The time came when there was not a thing in the house: no money, not even bread or milk or butter, or the inevitable Englishman's tea. So we decided that at meal-times, instead of going down to the dining-room, we would meet in the living-room, and have our meals by feeding on the Lord! But it never once happened, all through a week of having nothing.

Every day, three times a day, the bell rang just when we would be getting ready to meet upstairs, and down in the dining-room we would find bread, cheese, tea, milk and sugar. We never knew where they came from, and could only surmise from our cynical friend, Muss! On the eighth day there was a ring at the door-bell as we were eating; a man was outside and inquired if this was the Grubbs' house. He had a load of a ton of potatoes from a farmer who had recently heard of us and sent these along. It was certainly Hallelujah boys who carried those sacks in! Other provision came soon also and things returned to normal. But we always said anyhow God had given us extra, because the prayer is for daily bread, but we had cheese on top.

That same farmer, Warren Andrew, became a dear personal friend; he and his brother Will (both now with the Lord) and their sisters, especially Eleanor, have been a family whose love and friendship and constant visits to their home have been outstanding in our lives. Warren sent us sacks of lentils through those early years. Often they were our main diet, and sometimes we used to laugh and compare ourselves to the Israelites when it said the quails were so abundant they came out of their nostrils!

Once I was leaving home for a few days of meetings. We were just our own family of five at that time, and maybe one or two others. Before I left I asked Pauline what food or money she had. She said no food and 4s. (50c.) in cash. So we prayed and I left her, like any good husband, humanly to starvation, while I went to plenty! I hadn't left the house more than an hour or two, when a van drove up from a very highbrow West End store, Barkers. It contained a large hamper, not of luxury foods but of the basics: a joint of meat, packets of cheese, butter and so forth, and at the bottom a box of chocolates for "The Grublets". We had no idea where it came from.

After my return, we visited by invitation two friends in an apartment in Kensington, not far from Barkers. Our hosts were the two I have just mentioned, Will and Eleanor Andrew, brother and sister. At that time, we had only met them twice before. While we were there, Will took Pauline aside and asked her if she received a hamper of food on a certain day. Then he explained that as he was having his quiet time that morning, a voice had distinctly said to him, "Go to Barkers and order ample provision for a number of ordinary meals, and send it to the Grubbs."

I remember once when I was visiting my friend Rees

Howells, I was to go on in two days to some meetings in a town about 200 miles away. I had only a sixpence in my pocket, but I felt sure God would send some money for the fare, probably by a letter. No letter came, but I knew I should stick to my appointment, and the money for the ticket would come somehow. On the way to the station with Mr. Howells, we stopped at the post office and there was one letter—for him. We arrived at the station, and he remained at the back with my bag while I went to the booking office. I had by then a shilling or two more, and what I intended to do was to ask how far that amount would take me. But being accustomed just to ask for a ticket to a place, I mentioned the place and asked for the ticket. Immediately I saw I was caught, and here the man was clipping the ticket. As he did so, and was handing it to me through the window, a hand reached over my shoulder and a voice said, "Here, pay the ticket with this," and there was a pound note. It was Mr. Howells. I said nothing, but wrote and told him later. He then told me that he also had nothing, but there was a pound in that letter. He thought he would slip that pound into my hand when we shook hands as the train left; but instead the Lord's word came plain to him, "Go up to the booking office and put down that pound for the ticket." That was as narrow a squeak as I have had.

Pauline and I have not had a hard time. In fact, in recent years I have often told the Lord we have far too good a time, and He had better tighten it up on us. The tighter days were our years in England, because, though it has much changed now in this respect, English Christians were more accustomed to give to a mission than to individuals; so personal gifts were rare.

My first experience of receiving a personal gift when on a deputation tour was in the earlier days when we still had an English committee, and I was on furlough. I was sent for a six months' tour of Canada in 1929. I was just then learning and kind of experimenting in the personal life of faith, and I asked the Committee for permission to take no travel funds and to trust the Lord to supply *en route*, sending home for the work any gifts, and looking to the Lord directly for travel expenses. They did not like it too well, and felt the mission would be let down if I was caught somewhere penniless; so they insisted on my taking anyhow £5. The crisis moment came for me in Winnipeg, when I had money I could send home for the work, but none for my fare on to Regina that night. I was tempted to use the money. But to cut off the temptation, I took the money down to the post office, got a money order and posted it.

As I put the letter in the mail-box, a car drove up and in it was the treasurer of the church where I had been speaking, and he said he was wanting to see me to give me a generous cheque for the mission and another for my travel needs—$85: a fortune at a moment like that, especially as I had never before in my life received a gift like that.

The tour finished with all supplied, and as I boarded the ship to return from Montreal, a friend put a £5-note in my hand (or its equivalent). So I was able to return to the Committee the £5 they had made me take!

Of course, there is no doubt that those of us who do travelling and speaking are in a more advantageous position than those behind the scenes at the various Headquarters; and we do receive more. Often those at the home-bases, and indeed very often those on the fields, are scraping the bottom of the barrel. At our various Headquarters the family eats communally, though any are free to take their meals separately if they wish to, and usually couples with families do for breakfast. There is a kitchen purse, and we have always made it an aim of faith among ourselves that we should each put 10s. or $2 (or whatever is today's equivalent) in the purse each week. We have always made it clear to the candidates for the fields that if they are to prove the Lord on the fields, it is good they should prove Him at least in this small way weekly at home. But there has never been any further pressure or publicity, so no one is embarrassed or exposed if they do not contribute, because no one knows.

Once a week we share at the morning meeting how God is

providing for the household, with both thanksgiving and faith. We can only say it is marvellous. Through all these years in all these twenty-one main or regional headquarters, scattered through the home-base countries, not to speak of the training centres, the children's homes, the youth work, the C.L.C. headquarters, the *Soon* and *Bientôt* headquarters, the printing presses, Radio Worldwide, God has daily fed and clothed all their occupants without using mission funds, and provided for their children and their education often to college level. This is a thirty-eight-year miracle.

There are ways and means by which God provides. I am not sure of details in present-day Britain, but in the generous and prosperous U.S.A. there are supermarkets who load wrapped bread, cakes and so forth on us if we send a truck down—which we do. There are vegetables which can be bought for very little, fresh but unsold at the weekend. There are generous givers who send turkeys at Thanksgiving and Christmas. And as for clothes, there is a room set apart for all that come in, men's, women's and children's, and often lovely things (though also some not so lovely), so that home-basers or missionaries on furlough can restock. Few of us have bought new clothes for a long time. Sometimes when someone has died, a load of beautiful things comes from a kind relative. So all I can say is that, though in earlier days in Britain and doubtless also today, and elsewhere also, there were and are the tight times and food shortages, it very seldom looks like that at the daily meal tables.

BRANCHING OUT BY FAITH

The overseas home-bases, each autonomous, and not one senior to the other, but co-operating on an equal level in opening and reinforcing the fields, started, so far as our new day was concerned, when Alfred Ruscoe crossed to North America in 1934. There had been some footing for the W.E.C. in North America previous to that, and a few Americans and Canadians, especially the latter, in Congo. But it had almost come to a standstill when Alfred went out.

Alfred, small of stature, not strong in body, by no means the impressive heavy-weight, is both W.E.C.'s comic and one who knows and has practised the walk of faith more daringly and successfully than most of the rest of us. Just like the Lord again. I have already told how his life was overturned through his contacts with Rees Howells. I also mentioned how close in spirit we always have been. We drifted apart quite a bit through differences of opinion in the management of W.E.C. affairs. I think our correspondence in the growing days of W.E.C. in the U.S.A. and Canada often, unrealized by me, was quite oppressive to him, and he would feel I was trying to do some long-distance managing! But when together, on my fairly frequent visits, we always "clicked" in the things of the Spirit, and were adventurers together in the pursuit of God.

The outcome has been the U.S.A. and Canadian head-headquarters in Fort Washington, Pennsylvania, and Toronto; regional headquarters in Charlotte, North Carolina, for the south, and Portland, Oregon, for the west; eight new fields opened; as large a number of workers on the fields as from Britain, and a considerably larger financial provision. The main headquarters at Fort Washington, with its thirty-room mansion built by its wealthy owner like an imitation Scottish castle, and outbuildings of the same stone structure which make the office departments, standing in its 70 acres of grounds, was the biggest in the Crusade until the Lord gave us its brother in 1968 in Bulstrode. The C.L.C. has developed 20 acres as its own headquarters with offices, bookstore and ample accommodation for the staff, all built by specific acts of the obedience of faith before the money was in hand. The whole W.E.C.–C.L.C. community number around seventy.

No one can tell a faith story like Alfred Ruscoe, and many have been entranced and blessed, and laughed until they were sore listening to him; and no idle silly tales, but the real meat of the adventurous walk with God coming through the fun. He has retired from leadership now, though not from W.E.C.

activity. I am glad his memoirs are also just coming out. I have been refreshed by reading them, and so will anybody. The foolishness of God is wiser than men and the weakness of God stronger than men. It was a right guidance which made me invite him to rejoin us at that Liverpool meeting, as much a shock to me as to him; it was an equally right guidance that made me ask him to go out and reopen Canada and the U.S.A. to W.E.C., and that we would not give him an ounce of support. Once he started out, he was on the high seas with God, and that would be that. It gave him a kind of nervous breakdown for a few months, but by faith out of weakness he was made strong. He went, and these thirty years have been the rich outcome.

Australia was the next. A young man, Arthur Davidson, was a new recruit in Colombia, Latin America, not long after Pat Symes had started the work there. I was on a visit to Pat and the field, and this young man had the effrontery to say that he believed God was calling him back from the field to found an Australian headquarters for W.E.C. We weren't used to young recruits suggesting home posts for themselves! It looked too much like running away. So Pat and I said no. But so far from running away, he kept running after us. Pat and I visited some near-by town, and as we walked through the park, here was Arthur who had followed us to press his point once again. And once again, no. But whether by God or auto-suggestion (I am teasing, I know it to be of God), Arthur was found to need a severe operation and came to the States for it. We gave up. His health would have been a question mark.

He married his fiancée, Lillian, remained with Ruscoe for a year to learn more of headquarter ways and then started out. What made it worse, he was not even an Australian but a New Zealander! But it has been the same story: steady building, a maturing in Arthur himself as in all of us, for Arthur is a strong-viewed person and can make his views felt; but I never had any major clash with him; I think we always respected and loved each other, even when we differed. I had one grand visit to Australia and New Zealand and saw for myself some of what God was doing.

Australia of all our home-bases has most perfectly covered its field, with a string of regional headquarters stretching from Perth, through Adelaide and Melbourne, to Sydney which is the main headquarters, and on up to Brisbane. I think there has been less change of personnel and better stabilization than in any of our other home-bases. Amazing that thinly populated Australia with New Zealand has sent over a hundred missionaries to W.E.C. and C.L.C. fields. Money has been more of a battle. Australia is prosperous but I don't think its people are as free givers, anyhow as Americans.

New Zealand, those two beautiful and very English islands, has also done well. I visited my friend, Alec Thorne, who had opened the work in Spanish Guinea, West Africa, and later took over the representation of W.E.C. in New Zealand. A council had on its own represented us, of whom some still remain with us, such as Jim Mitchell, the Treasurer, and his wife. We had two months' travel together in Alec's car and many meetings. I loved the beauty of the mountain range we crossed in the southern land, and the fascinating hot springs in the north. Ivor Davies took over from Alec. Ivor, who was the "Mr. Ten" of those first ten, had a revolutionary experience himself at the time of the great outpouring of the Spirit on the Congo field, which has given him a ministry in the power of the Spirit; he helps to keep us through W.E.C. sensitive to the dangers of over-organization blocking those fresh breezes which come like the wind, no man knowing coming whence or whither going.

David Batchelor, a Scot, tough-looking as you would expect a Scot to be, once a footballer, is the kind of fellow you wouldn't like to exchange punches with; yet, as we know the real Scots are, full of humour with the laugh that makes you want to laugh with him, gentle, tender in spirit and a deep thinker. He has been in the van among us in thinking through the implications of this new era of missions, and has brought into being our inner-circle magazine, the *Weccor*, where we thrash out our varied viewpoints. With his Scottish wife, Chrissie, he was God's surprise choice for opening Continental Europe to us, not as a mission field, but for enlisting recruits. Starting in Spartan conditions in the top flat of a farm in Alsace Lorraine, having been refused permission to settle in Switzerland, he laid the foundation of a home-base in Switzerland which has now been in operation some years. A little committee was already at work there with a few faithful friends, and these were later joined by Heini Schyner and his wife Jo, who had been missionaries in China, and being Swiss could live in the country.

David then centred his attention on Germany, becoming expert in the language. A house and grounds big enough for a national headquarters became available near Frankfurt. Believing this to be God's provision, they took the usual step of faith and bought it, given three years to make the payment and, as usual, they proved the faithfulness of God. To Germany have been added a centre in Holland and another in Sweden. From Germany especially, but also from Holland and Switzerland, have been coming a good stream of recruits, now on nearly 100. What is it about the German character which produces a solidity and reliability? Perhaps that is why a Scot has had such success among them! But I say, Give us all the Europeans you can, and above all Germans. I can say nothing but nice things about David, because we have always hit it off together, since they made their first neophyte blunders in attempting to start a Manchester home-base. That headquarters has disappeared, but the lessons learned have borne their rich fruit on the Continent.

FIRST STEPS TO MANY NEW FIELDS

My world tours have covered many of our fields, though not all. The first visit I made to any field was by the Committee's request to Amazonia in 1928, soon after our first pioneer there, that tremendous Fenton Hall, had died in the forests. I spent six months there and found the going up those Amazon tributaries far tougher than anything I have experienced anywhere else in the world: paddled by Indians day after day up the forest-fringed river Pindare, a minor tributary, eaten by the pium fly during the day, and the mosquitoes by night when I had torn a hole in the net around my hammock, living on monkeys we shot and the voracious piranha fish we hooked, together with a manioc compound which looks like grapenuts, but must be soaked first or it will swell in the stomach and you will explode. The end of that journey was where Pat Symes and Fred Roberts (one of the three Freds later martyred) lived in an isolated village of Indians and had a few converts.

The real object of the visit was to suggest to the Committee who, out of the group of young missionaries, would be most suitable as field leader. My recommendation was Leonard Harris, which the Committee approved. The Amazon work passed over to become a field of the Unevangelized Fields Mission; but the warm link we always had with Len Harris has meant that, as he became British secretary of that mission, there has been real fellowship and brotherhood between us.

Naturally Congo was and is my first love. I had one six months' visit there in the early fifties. Of course a thrill to me, and with maturer years, I found how easy it was to love and find fellowship with the brother Africans. What changes! I mean spiritually. Jack Harrison, who had followed C.T., had led the way into the full recognition of the young national churches as self-governing churches of Christ, at that great series of Ibambi conferences in the early thirties. As many as twelve thousand from fifteen tribes mingled for a week, some coming journeys of weeks on foot, at first regarded with suspicion and then amazement by the Belgian officials that there could be such gatherings without inter-tribal conflict.

I had two priceless days with Jack when he was on furlough. He asked if we could be just by ourselves, and I was able to arrange for him to come to my mother's home. We went to the bottom together of what the New Testament church is, and our responsibility to recognize its full New Testament rights, no matter if some missionaries might drag their feet. It was not long before the Lord took that greatest of our missionaries, and I treasure the memory of those days we had together and their value. We had our patches of "outs" with each other, because I inadvertently put my fingers into some things which were field affairs and not my business, and it was good for me to be reminded that W.E.C. started in the heart of Africa, and we home-basers were their children, not their parents!

With Jack's successor, Jack Scholes, and his wife Jessie (as indeed with Jack Harrison's wife, Mary), we have had deepest unsullied fellowship all the years. We had a bond of confidence by which we could write to each other things we could not share more widely.

My visit was a year before the tremendous outbreak of the Spirit which for two years swept the area, maybe 500 miles by 300, and has been described in the booklet, *This is That*. That baptism of fire was a preparation for the baptism of suffering the churches and missionaries have now been through. Some of both Africans and missionaries have won the martyr's crown, others of the missionaries bear the scars in their bodies or memories of cruelties, humiliations and sufferings for Christ. Hundreds of the African brethren hid in the forests, nearly starved, but kept the banner of Christ flying high, sometimes at risk of life witnessing to their persecutors. Now they are back out from their hiding-places, praising God for His goodness and faithfulness, often left with only what none could take from them—Jesus in their hearts. The congregations are re-forming, the Bible School reopened, the missionaries welcomed back and many of the unsaved turning to the Lord.

My other journeys have taken me to Colombia, Latin America, as I have already mentioned; to India and Pakistan; to Indonesia, Java, Sumatra and Borneo; to Thailand, Korea and Japan. I am sorry that I never visited our West African fields, to their disappointment as well as mine. My primary links with these many fields had been in first gleaning the information of these areas that needed entry, often through the World Dominion Surveys published by my brother Kenneth; then at the home-base recognizing each as a specific commission from God and accepting the commission by faith; then the coming forward of the first volunteers for each, and giving whatever help and guidance we could about obtaining entry and establishing the first centre.

Knowing what it meant even to be faced with the entry of a new field, and then to see the entry become a fact, makes me laugh now when the newer workers speak so concernedly about the fields where there may now be twenty or so workers, churches, evangelists, translators and what not, as if practically nothing has been done, and look at the shortage of reinforcements and the great needs! Almost as if we are half asleep and had better awake to the fact that there is that field with these needs! Such is youth in every generation and it is good they are like that: and such is the quiet laugh of old age!

It was often only some extra push which got us going. In 1931 when in our desperate weakness we were just starting again with the Ten for Congo, I don't think I should have considered another field but for a challenge from our great friend and adviser, John D. Drysdale, the founder and principal of the Emmanuel Bible College, Birkenhead (from which we received over a hundred of our recruits in the early thirties, and delighted in their strong emphasis on the necessity of an experience of entire sanctification in addition to justification). When he said to me, "Why don't you go into Colombia, the least occupied republic of Latin America?" "Oh," I thought, "impossible in our condition." But it stuck with me and was confirmed when Pat Symes came along and told us how God had equally directed his attention there against his will.

India we were interested in through the news of the many movements among the outcastes. There came along a woman doctor, Katherine Harbord, who had been on the Nepal border and was set on returning alone to an isolated spot considered so dangerous that her mission would not send her. This was the kind that suited us, and she along with Dr. Wilfrid and Nancy Morris became our jumping-off point into our many-sided ministries in India and Pakistan.

Indonesia, as the Netherlands East Indies, had always been an objective from Mrs. Studd's day; indeed, before I went to Congo, Gilbert Barclay had asked me if I would not consider going to New Guinea. With the opening door, after independence, I and others of us put it to Harold Williams, one of our experienced Congo missionaries, then on furlough in Australia, to consider going to the island of Borneo. After no light heart-searching, he and Alice, his wife, saw it to be God's calling and went. But his greatest act of maturity was to give encouragement to a young Swiss, Heini Germann, of the type that no one could hold down, when he jumped across from Borneo to Sumatra and then into Java, which has opened up one of the greatest harvest fields in the W.E.C. of today. But Heini made these moves under a fire of criticism. Why didn't he stay put and dig his heels into the tribal work in Borneo? And if he did go to Sumatra, how could it possibly be God's will for him to leave that seed barely begun to be sown, and move into Java?

This was an excellent illustration of the way a crusade can become static, if it doesn't make room for pioneers whose actions are bound to appear out of line with those who are doing the more established work; and when there is a leader big enough to back the unusual, as was Harold. I think a real revelation of God to which we respond by the obedience of faith is always individual and tested by opposition more from the nearest to us than from those farther away; and the proof of a God-implanted faith is that we *must* fulfil it. The necessity is to have a fellowship flexible enough to let the weird ones go their weird way, even though many or most can't see it. If it is a mistake, God is good at giving us a judicious bump which hurts, but not too much! Heini's

148

most important work in Java was to bring into being the Batu Bible School under Indonesian leadership, the missionary staff working under an Indonesian council. This has been the dawning for us of the new day in missions when the foreign society disappears and is reborn as an arm of Christ's church in that country. This has been the most God-sealed action in W.E.C. since the Congo Revival. From the Bible School teams of students scatter out over the islands. In the Island of Timor alone the revival has swept in eighty thousand souls with healings, manifestations of the Spirit and dozens of local teams of witness; and in Sumatra something of the same. This mighty work of God, however, has met with continual opposition from some within our missionary ranks in the island, because the Bible School is linked with the established church in Indonesia, a product of the former Dutch Reformed Church.

Do we thus compromise our principles by contacts with ecumenical churches? Most of us believe that, while retaining our own status as a conservative evangelical crusade, we should co-operate with all who desire and offer us co-operation: just as already we owe many benefits to the brotherly assistance of missionaries and missions of the older denominations. Some of these have used their influence to get us into a country, such as the Rev. A. Allan of the Presbyterians in Colombia. Others have ministered to our needs in their hospitals and in other ways. Rather we thank God that while some interpret their calling to be come-outers from the older churches, or missions, others remain in them, maintaining their allegiance to the Scriptural faith of their foundations.

THE NEW TESTAMENT CHURCH IN INDIA

What impressed me most on my Asian visit was my eight days with Bakht Singh of India and his co-workers and congregations. Here was to me a sample of the coming world-wide church of Christ, where every nation has its own anointed men of God, its self-supporting and self-propagating churches, which in due course will begin to send witnesses to all parts of the earth, just as much as the churches of the West send their witnesses to other lands.

These churches in connection with Bakht Singh (he does not like us to call them Bakht Singh churches) have been born out of revolt against the India churches which so often have a profession of Christ, but not a possession. Bakht Singh has found their big snare to be "birthright membership", based on infant baptism; so that he is uncompromising about this. All who hear the Word through his witness, or the wide-spreading witness of the five hundred or so churches, receive immersion when there is clear evidence of the new birth, whether they have been previously "sprinkled" or not. Of course, this brings him in opposition to most of the established churches and, indeed, missions in India. I was surprised and shocked to find how the evangelical missionaries I met froze when I spoke of him, and accused him of being anti-white. But the truth is that he is not anti-white, but anti-death when it goes by the name of life, no matter what the colour of the skin.

I am bound to have sympathy with him in this stand he takes, because though I have never joined another denomination, having been brought up in the Church of England, I am as convinced as he that baptism for infants is not the baptism of the Scriptures and ensnares many into an illusory idea that they are Christ's. Yet having said this I immediately have to admit how much bigger God is than our limited concepts. Millions of His redeemed people believe in infant baptism as firmly as I disbelieve it! But, of course, I should have no interest in Brother Bakht Singh if water baptism was the main drive of his message. No, indeed. Here are people who are taught that true baptism is not in the flesh but spirit, in Romans 6 identification with Christ in death and resurrection, which is as much the gospel as Romans 3 justification.

There is no paid ministry. There are some who are set apart for ministry, but without salary. The young churches are taught to be witnesses in their towns, getting people around cups of tea, India's national drink; and as some show response, a team will visit, if so led after prayer for guidance, and after the team, some may remain to give further instruction; so new churches are formed.

We found such oneness of spirit with them, when I went for my visit by the encouragement of Wilfrid and Nancy Morris who were working with him, that I was enthusiastic for the suggestion that others of the W.E.C. staff give themselves to a teaching ministry in these young churches. I could by no means go along with the critics who seemed more disturbed about disrupting a dead Christianity than backing a living movement of the Spirit. Bakht Singh was thankful for any help W.E.C. could give of this kind, and some in W.E.C. were ready to respond.

The result has been an unbroken co-operation for about fifteen years, women workers among the women, a couple on children's work. We don't have many bachelors in W.E.C., but two of the few give themselves wholly to these churches, living on the Indian level, and that is no light thing in Indian villages or small town life—Noel Crocker and John Kennedy. Bill and Ena Pethybridge, older workers already mentioned from our British home-base, do the same. It was a big step, in middle age and never having been on a mission field, but has been the greatest success. The fact that there had always been an unusually sacrificial element in their daily living for Christ doubtless prepared them for this. As a result they are now getting after all of us oldsters to return to the front lines!

To us Westerners, the most striking part of the whole work with Bakht Singh are the Holy Convocations held annually at Hyderabad. We are so used to seeing younger churches on the mission fields, sincere and ready to move forward, but where is the money? "You Westerners must supply that." But Brother Bakht Singh puts on these Holy Convocations yearly where four thousand people are massed together in close quarters and all fed by the Lord for a week with no appeals to man, and in addition another two or three thousand who are daily visitors. Here is an Indian proving God exactly as we others do.

Bakht Singh has widened through the years in his relationships with the other churches of Christ. When I first met him, his separation from the denominations was rigorous; but later he linked with Billy Graham, and was on the platform not only with Billy but also with the Bishop of Madras, both of them, I am told, leading in prayer. But in all my missionary experience I think these churches on their New Testament foundations are the nearest I have seen to a replica of the early church, and a pattern for the birth and growth of the young churches in all the countries which we used to talk about as the mission fields.

We are in this new era of missions, though I am only on the outer edge of it, having now retired from being secretary of W.E.C. But I see it as a thrilling new day for the whole church of Christ. The political upheavals have as usual been God's convenient agent for taking us a stage further in "the good pleasure of His will". All countries, or nearly all, have thrown off the yoke of subservience and control by others. In nearly all the infant church was in existence, but dependent upon us Western missionaries. Now they are rising up, and just as politically they are right in saying, "We are as good as you," so God's people of all races and colours can say, "We are brethren, and we may be ministers of Christ to you as much as you to us." Already there are national missionary societies in Japan, the Philippines, Korea, India, Indonesia, and doubtless others, to take the gospel to other lands outside their own.

In our own ranks, as our Survey Secretary, Leslie Brierley has been calling us on to an entire re-examination of our missionary policies. Leslie's early schooling did not fit him for this. He was one of our two pioneers into Senegal. In war years he was in government service in Sierra Leone where he began to find a liking and aptitude for survey work. On his return to England he applied this aptitude to producing in great detail surveys of Africa, India and other lands, pinpointing areas of special need. Married to Bessie Fricker, the woman pioneer to Portuguese Guinea, the two of them with their co-workers gave birth and early nurture to the churches there. Now back as Survey Secretary he produced for us what we call our Nineteen Point Programme of new and difficult fields to be entered, a dozen of which now have a first entry, including Chad, the Trucial States, Sardinia, Mozambique, Gambia, Iran. But more than that, his challenge to us has been the rethinking of missions in this modern era in terms of the absorption of the local W.E.C. into the national churches, or partnership with them; and the enlargement of our ranks to include crusaders of other nationalities, or help in training national missionaries for their own national missionary societies.

Leslie and I have been close through the years; indeed, we have always been like father and mother to him and Bessie. So to me it has been a great thrill to see God mould and develop him along these unexpected lines—from effective pioneer to a recognized authority among missions on missionary strategies for our day, and almost as a paratrooper among us, parachuting down to unentered areas and calling us on to accompany him. What hidden gifts come to the surface when God has charge of a life.

THE KEY TO LIFE IN RUANDA

During my Congo visit, Jack Scholes and I were invited to take a 500-mile journey over the intervening mountain range to Ruanda in East Africa and have a fortnight with the brethren there.

What has become known as the Ruanda Revival or East African Revival already has its place in the history of revivals. It has been one of the great movements of God's Spirit in this century. The brethren themselves do not like it being called a "revival". They don't like any term which draws attention away from Jesus Himself, the Person, to an "event" which can be examined or imitated or analysed down to a set of principles. They say, and rightly, that Jesus is

revival, because the word only means re-viving, a renewed
life; and life is Jesus in the heart. Revival therefore is not
some necessarily cataclysmic outburst of the Spirit, but
people walking daily in a cleansed and living relationship
with Jesus and one another.

We had heard from Edith Moules, our pioneer leprosy
worker in the Congo, of the revolutionary change in her
life and ministry through contacts with Ruanda brethren
(a story which has been told in the biography I wrote of her—
Edith Moules, Mighty Through God); so I had invited two of
the missionaries, Joe Church and Bill Butler, to visit us in
London for two days. This was followed later by a visit from
two of the Africans, William Nagenda and Yosiya.

Both visits had a definite impact of the Spirit upon us.
Their humility, simplicity and naturalness made a first impression. This was particularly striking in the African
brethren, because this was their first visit to a Western
country. Here they were, landed from a plane among fifty
whites; yet there were no "airs", neither too much put on,
nor taken off, just two brethren detached from self because
walking with Jesus. The hours spent with those fifty of us
were in simple fellowship, using the Scriptures with personal
application to their own experiences, telling of how God had
worked in their own lives up to date, and among the African
brethren. Opportunity was given for any of us to participate,
and some did. I particularly remember two of our number,
David Batchelor and Ken Adams, saying how directly God
had spoken to them about incidents in their personal lives,
and the touch from God made a permanent impact on them.
The two Africans made their home with us as they toured
the country, and typical of their simple walk in the light was
what they told us on one occasion. Yosiya is an ordained
clergyman and William a layman (the lay–clergy differentia-
tion which has been established in most denominations, but
which I don't believe was in the early church or Scriptures);
Yosiya was slow with his English, but William could speak
fluently. Yosiya told us how he began to be jealous of

William, the layman, when he could see how people gravitated around him. This put a barrier between them until Yosiya got into the light, shared this with William and all was buried in the blood of Christ; and they wanted us to share in the liberty and unity they now enjoyed.

Every new moving of the Spirit takes some new form, and has both its adherents and critics. For myself, I began to see that what God was doing in Ruanda, and has continued to do, and which has spread to thousands around the world, is restoration at the heart of normal church life of the free fellowship type of meeting—the house groups when "they that fear the Lord speak often one to another", and when the often quoted "not forsaking the assembling of ourselves together" is given the full content of that statement which goes on to say "*but exhorting one another*". Not the preacher–congregation relationship, the one speaking, the others silent: not the teacher–taught: but where all are free to participate if they want to, and where the participation is from personal experience, sharing some light received, some Scripture applied to daily living, some happening where the Lord meets a need or restores a lapse.

The class meetings of the early Methodists, which were the heart-beat of the young congregations, were of this kind. The tremendous impact on thousands of Frank Buchman and the Oxford Group, especially among the up-and-outs, in their early years was the same: face the four absolutes—absolute honesty, purity, unselfishness and love: confess, repent, receive forgiveness through Christ; hand yourself over to the control of God; listen for God's guidance, record it and follow it; share with others what God has done for you, and challenge them to the same honest relationship with God.

To my mind, though I never had close personal contact with them, this was the greatest move of God's Spirit in the twenties and early thirties of our century. How many I have met whose lives were transformed through their Oxford Group contacts. The criticism has been valid, I think, when they changed to calling themselves Moral Rearmament

155

(M.R.A.), that they no longer make redemption through Christ central to their message; and this has meant an almost total severance from the Christian church. But I also think that much criticism was invalid in those early days, when it centred on supposedly lurid and embarrassing sin-confessions. I think for many that was an escape from readiness to bring our own lives into the light, and meet with our fellow-men at the foot of the cross, ready maybe to admit sins way back in the past, but much less ready to admit the daily failures and daily need of forgiveness and cleansing.

What God had now begun to do again in the later thirties in Ruanda and in East Africa was really a repetition of this same working of the Spirit, on the fellowship, horizontal level, walking together in the light and challenging others to do the same. The East African Brethren would repudiate any implication that they have a family resemblance to the early Oxford Group, because their emphasis is so altogether Jesus and His cleansing blood, whereas the Oxford Group even in their beginning days never made Him so central. Yet in fact these same ways of the Spirit have taken renewed form in these brethren. They have been the key to the effectiveness of their world-wide witness, because I believe honest fellowship has been the way of the Spirit from the birth of the church, and must find recurring means of expression.

Ruanda has been under the same fire of, I believe, unjustified criticism—that there is too much sin-confessing. Even our own Congo field missed a blessing in this respect, I believe, because reports were brought back from two of our women missionaries who visited Ruanda. They had not liked some references by some lady to her unfulfilled desire in not being married, and in the fellowship where they used a form of embrace in which one greets another by putting an arm around him, some African brother had done that to a missionary lady. As a result, the suggestion of a team of Africans and missionaries visiting our field was turned down.

But I had seen, as I have said, the obvious change in our Edith Moules, the founder of our leprosy fields, after she had been in Ruanda at the time her husband, Percy, went to be with the Lord. The quality of the fellowship life between Africans and missionaries in the brokenness and openness, the joy in cleansing, the sharing and ultimate personal challenge by an African had such a searching effect on her that it made her see, in her own ministry with a thousand leprosy patients, her pointing finger at their inconsistencies, but never the other three fingers pointing back at herself and her quick temper. The sharing of this with her leprosy patients which produced such changes in them, then the changes in her we could all see on her return to London, and then the visits of the brethren to us in London already mentioned, made me want to meet with the brethren in Ruanda myself, when I was visiting our Congo field. Because I knew some were critical, I did not feel I could make the visit until after I had been on our field; but I was grateful that Jack Scholes was keen for us to go together.

I can only say that the effect of those two weeks was not to make a critic of me, but a thankful recipient of much from God to myself. I did not find unhealthy emphasis on sin-sharing, but an altogether healthy and glorious emphasis on cleansing and liberation in the blood of Jesus, coming out in their continuous repeated theme song "Tukutendereza" (Glory, glory Hallelujah, glory glory to the Lamb), and the joy of the daily walk in the light with Him. Roy Hession was out there at that time also. His little book, *Calvary Road*, has brought to hundreds of thousands what God gave us there. I followed it by another small brochure, *Continuous Revival*, published by the Christian Literature Crusade and still in circulation.

In W.E.C. itself our contacts with the East African brethren have had an influence, quite apart from the various ones whose lives were specifically touched. The fellowship basis was not new to us; but the readiness to share from our daily lives became more a part of us. There has been no official adoption of some new way of fellowship. We are not meant to imitate each other, and this fellowship emphasis has been peculiarly a ministry to which the Ruanda brethren have been called. Ours is different. I think many Weccers would say that I have always had a tendency to pick up some new thing and run it as if there was nothing else, and I went through a phase of that through my Ruanda contacts. I used to have sessions in our London morning meetings for God's up-to-date dealings in our lives. They did not "catch on" as a permanency, though I still think there is a missing note among us in not having more up-to-date interchange. In recent years, in the U.S.A., I have become closely connected with others whose emphasis is group fellowship, in the wide-spreading fellowship known as *Faith at Work*, and once again the Spirit is moving among thousands across the country. But I will have more to say on this later.

One other effect of a visit to the East African brethren has greatly impressed me. This time in the life of a Negro-American, Ernie Wilson, who has been a friend of mine and of the W.E.C. for twenty years. Ernie is a minister in Phila-delphia, and is almost a part of the W.E.C., sharing in W.E.C. teams and a constant visitor among us. Five years ago some friends made it possible for him to visit the brethren in East Africa. The result was an absolute transformation. He knew the Lord before and preached Christ; but now it is a liberated walk with Jesus, sharing what He is in his daily life. It is not colour and race questions that bother him, but the simple solution for all, black and white: Jesus in the hearts and daily life, with constant repentance and cleansing when sin comes in, is unity between brethren "neither Jew nor Greek, barbarian, Scythian, bond nor free, but Christ is all, and in all". Doors world-wide are opening to him and his witness, in Africa, in the West Indies, in this country and now recently an invitation from the Premier of Alberta, Canada, to tour that province.

MY MINISTRY IN WRITING

Writing was the last thing I expected to do. I had no particu-lar training, and I am not literary. It is only in recent years that I have awakened intellectually, and though I now love reading and could spend my life at it, it is too late, and my knowledge of English literature is very slight. Poetry I know and love, but again too late to be a serious reader of it. I was forced, when at home around 1925, to take up the publishing of our W.E.C. magazine, because Gilbert Barclay who was then Home Overseer was ill. About my only idea was to select stuff which was lively and I thought would attract readers; and to cut out from field reports the clichés, the formal Scripture quotations, and the constant wearisome repetitions of "pray for so and so" whom the reader would never have heard of. The death in the Amazon forest of that great pioneer, former heavyweight officer boxer of the Royal Air Force, Fenton Hall, made me feel that there should be some printed record of him. His journals came home and they were vibrant, so I got to work editing them and they were published anonymously under the title, *Fenton Hall, Pioneer and Hero*. That was my first effort at publication, though not under my name. That little book has such a challenge that it still sells after forty years. Comments were made on its poor literary style, but I knew no better and don't now. Anyhow it had the bite of the Spirit about it.

After C.T.'s death came the need to have something written on him. Who could do that? The one I knew had the writing gift was his daughter Edith, Alfred's wife, but she wouldn't do it. So back it came to me. I made the find of my life when someone directed me to a tall cupboard in the cellar of No. 17, and in it I found all the records of his life from his first golden curl, his boyhood letters from Eton days, and right up to his African days. Tremendous, and his writings were as pungent as his living. Our friend, Mr. Fremlin, as I have already said, put me on a farm on the Scottish moor by myself, with abundant farm meals provided; and there I divided my time between reading, classifying, marking lively parts, and going refreshing walks in the silence of the moors. In a month I had it ready, and it was easy to dictate to Olive Moore, tying the various sections together by comments and explanations. That's the only way I have ever known to write a biography. God blessed it and it was an enormous success under the title, *C. T. Studd, Cricketer and Pioneer*. Lutterworth Press accepted it, and indeed went so far as to say it would be a modern *Pilgrim's Progress*. After thirty years I still meet people everywhere I go who tell me how their lives were changed through reading it. I believe it has been one of the great missionary biographies of the generation—twenty-one impressions in English, translations into about twelve languages.

Other biographies seemed needful: *Alfred Buxton*, C.T.'s co-pioneer; it was a token of love to prepare that; *Jack Harrison, Successor to C. T. Studd*; *Edith Moules, Mighty Through God*; *J. D. Drysdale, Prophet of Holiness*; *Rees Howells Intercessor*; *Abraham Vereide, The Modern Viking*.

Each of these went to several impressions and, except for the last two, then dropped. I still hope *Jack Harrison* can be republished because I think it is standard for young men to see what it means to be a dedicated missionary servant of Christ: the very opposite of C.T.—the one from a wealthy home, the other from the working-class district of Liverpool. Conditions may change, but quality of living never.

The only non-seller, which hardly went through its first edition, was *J. D. Drysdale*. I think the title *Prophet of Holiness* may have frightened readers off. It was the life story of the founder of the Emmanuel Bible College, Birkenhead, as I have already mentioned, who was a master trainer of missionary recruits; and Mr. Studd had particularly asked that we get trainees from him. He was also an intimate friend to me and often an adviser as an elder brother in Christ. I hold both him and Mrs. Drysdale in love and admiration. There were two "holiness" men whose names used to be linked together—J. D. Drysdale and wee George Hart, and I was proud to have intimate fellowship with them both, as now with J. D. Drysdale's daughter and son-in-law, Rhoda and Stanley Banks, who succeeded to the principalship of the College.

I also used the stories, usually dramas of faith and daring, of the entry into many of our new fields, to put together booklets of about 30 pages. There was *Mountain Movers* on Colombia; *Penetrating Faith* in Spanish Guinea (now Rio Muni); *Ploughing Through* on the Ivory Coast; *This is that* on the tremendous outpouring of the Spirit in Congo (though this was published anonymously); and *Concrete Evidence of faith that works* on the building by faith of the Hostel at our London Headquarters. Many of these sold in thousands because I felt that, not mundane facts of a field move the hearts of the average reader, but evidences of a God who still does the impossible through faith.

I also wrote two books of that kind: *After C. T. Studd* on the spread of the work to many countries and at the home-bases through faith; and *Christ in Congo Forests* (entitled *With C. T. Studd in Congo Forests* in its U.S.A. edition) to explain in more detail the spiritual principles on which the work on our mother field had been founded; also some of the battles involved in the birth and growth of a church of the Holy Spirit, and not merely of nominal professors. In later years also there has been a small book, *The Four Pillars of W.E.C.*, to keep before the newer generation the foundations upon which we are built.

The other type of book on the life in the Spirit started by a series of articles I wrote for our magazine, *Worldwide*, on the lessons we were learning at our morning meetings and how we applied them—knowing the will of God, faith, almighty meekness, the adventure of adversity, the released life—a 50-page book called *Touching the Invisible*. It was published in 1934, and has had a remarkably long life; it is still selling and circulating, and quite often people tell me what light it has brought them, and they still like it the best.

I don't know how I came to take the step of preparing for publication the first of the series of books seeking to examine and find the answer to what I put in the form of three questions: What is life? How do we live it? Why do we live it? The first of the five books was *The Law of Faith*, seeking to dig to the bottom of what faith really is and how we believe. The next was *The Liberating Secret*, on the key to the released life. The third, *The Deep Things of God*, on the law of opposites and how it helps to get life in focus when we have an understanding of this. The fourth, I think the clearest and most comprehensive of all, *God Unlimited*, where the heart of the matter is seen most clearly to be the One Person in the Universe, and we are an expression of Him. The fifth, *The Spontaneous You*, a further attempt in a more shortened form to cover these answers to these three basic questions. All five continue in circulation.

To tell the truth, I can't really differentiate clearly between what is said in the one or the other of these books. They are simply heart and mind outpourings at the time each was written, with the space of a year or two between each. I have never re-read the books, so I never attempted to build the next on to the previous one. Having written one from what was filling my thinking and satisfying my heart at the time, I then continued with my outer W.E.C. activities and inner pursuit of ultimate answers, until I began to feel again that in some further respect things were clearer, and there was something I should like to share, and which people seemed to want and was missing. And so the next would appear. So they were really heart and mind commentaries on what was going on inside me at that time, and having some effect on my life. I never wrote one as a kind of duty or "study", or because I felt I ought to hammer out something more. They were always from the freedom of wanting to share what had become great light to me, and I suppose I should add what I thought were missing gaps in normal evangelical teaching—and I must confess still think so.

As I say, I am no literary man. I never read a book on how to write, with one exception. Someone gave me Quiller Couch's paperback of a series of lectures given at Cambridge by him, "Q" as he was called. I was fascinated by them and their brilliance. I think the title was *The Art of Writing*, and I always regret having lost my copy and have never seen one since. I remember one lesson stuck with me—the difference between masculine and feminine writing: masculine being the active voice—"Someone told me"; feminine the passive—"I was told by someone"; and pointing out how continually both Shakespeare and the King James Version are in the active voice. The only writers I ever read with attention to their style are Shakespeare, only his riches overwhelm me, and Macaulay. I always love the great flow of his sentences. I know it is not fashionable today to use long sentences. People are too busy and active to pick up their meaning, I suppose; but I think Macaulay has influenced me as my ideal, and therefore I tend to use long ones also.

In spiritual writings I have been greatly influenced by William Law the Mystic (I will be saying much more about him). He also had this flow of magnificent English; but also I liked his way of explaining profound truth, pages of it, by straight logical examination of what he was presenting, and very little diversion into illustrations. I caught much the same in Paul's magnificent presentation of the depths of all truth, especially in Romans, but through all his letters with illustration or story-telling way in the background. I have modelled much on this, which I know makes the books heavy reading and mind-stretching, and often they would be better and easier with more windows for illustration. Others have told me that. But I never have been a born raconteur, and can never, for the life of me, remember a single funny story—a great lack! And so I can't change my skin when writing. Beyond this I have had nothing. I am sure any trained writer, particularly in these days of writing seminars, could pick a thousand holes in my style, grammar, punctuation, etc. One lady—I have not had the courage to answer her—sent me back a copy of *God Unlimited* with sentences underlined in nearly every page, and alternative better English. But as I read her alternatives, I still think they may have been more polished and correct, but they subtracted from the virility and liveliness of what I was saying in my own way. But perhaps that is a neat rationalization!

Lutterworth Press, the publishing agency of the United Society for Christian Literature, publishers with a top-class reputation throughout the Christian world and beyond, have always graciously accepted and published the books. It was they who encouraged me to write *C. T. Studd* and they have never withdrawn their encouragement since. I have only had to send them a manuscript and they have accepted it; and all the books they turn out are well produced. I have never once been less than pleased with any of them. Their range of publications include well-known books and authors in a wide spectrum of Christian thinking, wider than just the strict evangelical, though including them; so I have been glad to have a publisher whose books reached more than one sector of the Christian public. Because their interest is the spread of the Christian message, I have greatly appreciated the way they have been content for editions of a book to go slowly. I know busy publishers who just cut you off after an impression or two, if the book is not a quick seller. This has greatly helped me.

By arrangement with Lutterworth Press, all these books are published in the U.S.A. by our own folks, the Christian Literature Crusade of Fort Washington, Pennsylvania.

VI

*The Continuous Challenge
of Faith*

THE THIRD CRISIS OF MY INNER LIFE, WHICH I PUT ON A LEVEL
with the other two—of the new birth and the discovery of
Christ living in me, came unexpectedly. I do not know if I
can yet define it in exact terms. It was as radical and definite
in what I went through and in its outcomes, as the first two.
Perhaps I would call it my enlargement—from an inner
personal Christ to a universal Christ. I would liken it to the
expansion in Paul's prayer for the Ephesians (Eph. 3:16–19)
from being rooted and grounded in a personal love relationship with the indwelling Christ to the understanding of a
universal Christ of limitless dimension, encompassing all
earth with a love with no boundaries. Perhaps it was the
necessity of a mental enlightenment to keep pace with a
heart love. But its effect has been a vast enlargement of both
heart and mind.

It struck me like a cyclone. Pauline thinks it was just a
kind of breakdown through pressure of work. I am sure it
was not. I had only been W.E.C. secretary four years in
1935, and was just forty years old. I had begun to have a
thirst for enlarged understanding and deeper reading, the
kind of student mentality I should have had fifteen years
before. I could only be a dabbler in my busy life, but one
book I picked up was William James' *Varieties of Religious
Experience*. It hit me like a boxer's knock-out blow. That
itself is an evidence of my immaturity in thinking things
through; for as I read the psychological explanation of Paul's
conversion on the road at Damascus, it suddenly struck me
that perhaps this was only some inner change in Paul's
psychological make-up, and that there is no reason to postu-
late a divine revelation; and that perhaps there really is no

God—just the human race. I don't think James himself meant this if I had gone on to finish the book; but here was I, a missionary of fifteen years' standing, and a secretary of a missionary society, and I was questioning the existence of God. It may be laughable, or so obviously immature, but it hit me for six, to use cricket language. Life blanked out on me. I told Pauline, and I did try once to speak at a meeting for which I was booked, and it was simply hell—to speak of one whose existence I was doubting; and I told her I couldn't do it any more.

Pauline has a woman's courage. She never let on to me how she must have felt with the possibility of our life's work in ruins, and us wandering we knew not where; but she quietly said we would make arrangements to leave for a time and go visiting. Only one other in our mission ranks knew and he only because he caught a kind of Freudian slip when I was talking with him and added, "If there be a God." This was my gentle loving co-worker Jock Purves, who caught it that I was in an inner bind, said nothing to anybody, but just quietly took on the leadership for me.

I was a year away in different places, partly in a seaside home lent us on the coast at Southwold, which gave me plenty of chances of walking on those breezy sand dunes. We also went for a month to our loved Rees Howells. Pauline says that the only time she ever came near being hit was when she tried to explain to him that I was doubting the existence of God; he wiped the suggestion aside so vehemently that he raised his hand as if he could almost strike her. Of course she may have mistaken his meaning; but the point was his almost violent repudiation of the absurdity of such an idea, and his certainty that of course I didn't really believe such a thing.

My answer came through the mystics and has been widening ever since. I don't know who first put me on to them; but somehow there came into my hands a book called *Wholly for God*. It was nothing but extracts from the writings of William Law; but the subtlety of it was that it was edited by

168

Andrew Murray, who was and still is one of the stand-bys of the Keswick and "deeper life" movements, and his books are still widely used. So this put the imprimatur on it of his "soundness"; whereas if it was just a book of Law, the Mystic, some might be suspicious of it—such weird ideas folks have of what mysticism is. The book fascinated me. There was his beautiful English, admitting sometimes the complication of his long sentences. It wasn't that! It was the heights and depths he was opening to me of the nature of God, the real meaning of the fall, what God's wrath and mercy really are, what heaven and hell really are, and what atonement and the in-Christ relationship really is. I had never seen such heights and depths before. I drank and drank, although it took time to absorb. I then began to find that Law himself had been a legalistic idealist, knowing nothing of grace through faith, and in that stage of his experience had written his best-known book, *A Serious Call to a Devout and Holy Life*, which is straight Christian standards of living with no inkling of how to live them. It was that book which John Wesley had sought to follow in his Holy Club unenlightened days, and which put him off William Law, as though he was just a misguided legalist. Wesley never discovered what had happened to Law through his introduction to the one he always spoke of as "the Blessed Behmen".

It was Law's introduction to the German shoemaker of Görlitz, Jacob Boehme (Law always spelt it Behmen) which poured light into Law, and inspired him to write those two matchless treatises—*The Spirit of Love* and *The Spirit of Prayer*. I was able to get a set of Law's seven volumes which includes these two, and also includes his *Way to Divine Knowledge* and his *Address to the Clergy* which are almost equally as good. These carried me deeper and deeper into Boehme's marvellous unfolding of God and the universe. I was beginning to catch on to the answer in the source and unity of all things in the One. I was able to get most of Boehme's books which have been translated into English. *The Aurora, The Three Principles of the Divine Essence, The*

169

Threefold Life of Man, *The Mysterium Magnum* and the rest. I found a little bookshop in Cecil Court off Charing Cross Road, John M. Watkins, who carries this more eclectic type of book.

From Boehme, most difficult to read because he could not easily put the depths of his illuminations into readable form, I got my answer, and to this day know no writer to match him. He was no visionary, but in desperation because he could not reconcile God's wrath and mercy, received insights into the nature of God, the nature of being, the interaction of opposites (he got his first illumination by seeing sunlight glancing off a pewter vessel), which are true all the way to Scripture, but takes us into the depth of their underlying meanings. Christ incarnated, crucified, risen and glorified is central to him; but he gathered together into one all the apparently twisted strands of the meaning of life as no one else. He is a last word to me. How I revelled in him and Law. I get more from a sentence or two of Boehme, amidst much I can't understand, than from whole books of others.

Others of the great mystics helped—John of the Cross with his *Dark night of the Soul* and *Ascent of Mount Carmel*; Santa Teresa, Meister Eckhart, Henry Suso, John Tauler, John of Ruysbroeck, Walter Hilton, the author of the *Cloud of Unknowing* and the *Theologica Germanica*, Plotinus, Angelus Silesius, Richard Rolle, Lady Julian of Norwich. Also writers who help expound the mystics, especially Evelyn Underhill and William Kingsland, also Rufus Jones.

I have by no means confined my reading and searchings to the officially orthodox. I have to admit that I find great treasure in many writers who have cut loose from some of the fundamentals I adhere to, but who have special insights often missed by us in our stricter limitations; for the diamond of God's truth has just too many sparkling facets for any one pair of eyes. One of the earliest that opened much to me was a little book of unknown authorship called *Christ in you*. It is way off in some respects (an evangelical friend of mine returned the copy thoroughly marked with disapproving

170

comments), but is way on in some. William Kingsland's *Rational Mysticism*; Walter Lanyon's glowing interpretations of the unified life; and an anthology of poetry from which I get constant refreshment, the *Oxford Book of English Mystical Verse*. These are out of bounds to the orthodox; but I have often got more from them than from normal Bible exegesis. I see they could be dangerous for those who are not first rooted down and fixed in the Bible fundamentals of our faith. I have become so Bible-soaked that I instantly detect and react against and reject what I cannot line up with Scripture. I had a struggle at one time when I thought that some writers were not maintaining the distinction between the human self being essentially divine, which is false, and the human self losing its independent selfhood on the cross and finding its "divinity" in the indwelling Christ. But I came also to see that often I misjudged these writers as I dug deeper into what they were saying.

INTERPRETING THE CRISIS

I do not mean that I read all these at this time, I am rather gathering together some of the accumulation of writers that have helped to mould my understanding. The heart of the stabilizing revelation to me, and what has become the total answer to all life for me, has been that there is only One Person in the universe, and that the whole universe is His myriad forms of Self-manifestation. Of course I am immediately dubbed a pantheist and am often asked if I am. Those who ask that either don't understand what a pantheist is or don't understand what I am saying about my own beliefs. A pantheist, according to its Greek derivation, means that everything is God. I am saying that everything is a form by which He manifests Himself, much as my body is not exactly I, but an outward form of the inner me. This fact, gleaned through Boehme, confirmed through the writings of many others, and with the foundations in Scripture, has given me my anchor. It has moved me on from my separated concepts, and this I think is the weakness of evangelical teaching, of a

God apart from His creation "making" His creation, much as a carpenter appears to be apart from the table he makes.

That is why also I have sympathy, I know against the tide of my evangelical friends, with writers like Wren Lewis, the English scientist, in his marvellous little *Return to the Roots*, and Bonhoeffer, and the much opposed John Robinson. Some things I dissociate myself from, where any question the historicity of Bible fact and seek to distort it into myth; but I see where these men have an appeal today, because they answer the modern contention that we need not look without to an authority who from some vast distance made this world and laid down standards for living. The answers are found within—for the physicist in the atom; for the biologist in the cell; for the psychologist in the mind; for the sociologist in the inherent rights of man. Is there here an answer for the greatest inwardness, the human spirit in its rebellious self-centredness? Yes, when we discover the possibility of God as Spirit joined to the human spirit through Christ. For these men point out that God was from the beginning of time revealed as Spirit, confirmed by Jesus who said outright, "God is Spirit"; and Spirit is the Person within, as our human spirits are within our bodies.

So He as the author of the universe is the inner life of it. He "fills heaven and earth", therefore, is within them. He is to be finally revealed as what He really is—All in all, which leaves nothing but Himself. "The beyond in the midst", the Transcendent in the Immanent. And as the One Person in the universe, He can only manifest Himself as a Person by persons. So Jesus lived His human life, as the archetypal man, by the Father dwelling in Him (John 14:10), which was the startling surprise to His disciples who, in their separated human outlook, expected an external revelation, when they asked Him to show them the Father. And He went on to say that this was why He had come as redeemer, so that God the Spirit who was in Him would be God the Spirit in an inner unity with all who receive Him. And that was Pentecost; not the outward manifestations which were but a

172

means; but the end—an inner fixed consciousness of their union with Him—He in them—they in Him.

So here, as these writers point out, is the final answer to the human problem. If all resources for all things on all levels are found within, what final resources are there for the most inward of all—the human self? What solution for the insurmountable self-centredness of the human spirit which is the cause of all the human chaos? And here is the answer. Christ within. The Holy Spirit within. God dwelling in us: then in that realized union through free choice, in Christ's cross and resurrection, the human spirit of self-centredness is united to the divine Spirit of self-giving. "Dead to sin and alive unto God", man becomes a human expression of God who is love: a perfectly normal man in his perfectly normal environment with his normal human reactions and human weaknesses, yet God's strength so made perfect in weakness that it is not we living, but He by us; just as a branch is a normal expression of the life of the tree of which it is a member.

It is John who puts into one short phrase the character of this One Person in the Universe—God is love; and love means existing to meet the need of others, with total indifference to what happens to yourself. Love belongs to need, just as Jesus who was Love in the flesh, likened Himself to bread, which ceases to live its own life in a cornfield and finds its true end in being the means by which others live. All forms of creation demonstrate this to be so, and that they are involuntary manifestations of Him whose forms they are, because everything finds its true end in being something for others: the tree becomes a table for me, the metals in the earth become my conveniences for living. But God as the Person can only be a person through persons, so that in this living union in Christ, as He is limitless love, so we are love in endless variety of expression, for "as He is, so are we in this world".

But to be a person with limitless potential means conscious freedom. To be a person is to be conscious of endless variety

173

and to be capable of making choices from among the variety. Freedom is not being anything, but is freedom to make choices. All life is making choices, but the significance is that choices make destiny. I become what I choose. The law of choice, which is the same as saying the law of faith, is that what I take takes me. I take food. What I eat takes me! I choose a profession. I choose to become a carpenter, for instance. I apply myself and carpentry takes me over. Carpentry becomes my second nature, and I express my freedom in practising my carpentry. This is even said of Almighty God. How can the Scriptures say He is Almighty and then say there is something He cannot do? Because they do say so. Paul says, "God that cannot lie." It is because God is the First Self, and a conscious self makes choices, and there is one fundamental choice a self makes. Should he be a self-lover or a self-giver? A liar is a self-lover, and God "cannot" be that. He is fixed by His choice. He can only be love—the Other-lover, the Self-giver.

But we humans have been caught up in the opposite choice. Through the Fall, we became enslaved to the one who had become by choice the opposite to our God of love, Satan, the devil, once called Lucifer, who became fixed by his choice as the god (the originator) of self-centredness. According to the Bible, he, as the spirit of error, entered humanity (Eph. 2:2; 1 John 4:4 and 6), and took us captive, so that it is natural to us to be self-seekers and self-lovers. And how can we be rescued?

We have become stolen property, manifesting the character of the wrong god, and already reaping some of its poisoned fruits leading on to an eternal destiny of "everlasting destruction from the presence of the Lord and the glory of His power".

But love belongs to need, and God is love, and we are in need. Indeed, the character of love is that need has a claim on love. That is why Paul calls himself a debtor to take the gospel to the Gentiles (Rom. 1:14), because need is always the creditor which can claim payment from love the debtor.

And that is why we are told to love our enemies, because if I deliberately hurt you as your enemy, I hurt you outwardly, but I am hurt inwardly by my wicked intent. It is not the one hurt who is in need but the hurter: and love belongs to need. So God is hurt by our rejections of Him, not because we hurt Him but because we are hurting and damning ourselves. So, being love, He gives Himself to meet our need in the person of His Son, "God in Christ reconciling the world unto Himself and not imputing their trespasses unto them." What happens to Him is not the point. Love is unconditional, and if God must die at the hands of His enemies to save His enemies, then He will die.

So Jesus lays down His life on the cross, none taking it from Him except by His own choice, and God raises Him from the dead. The whole of Scripture interprets this for us as the judicial removal of the inevitable separation of the human race from God for eternity, which is the consequence of us being law-breakers (sinners), guilty, cursed, condemned. This was completed by Him Himself voluntarily taking the place of separation from God on the cross in our place, "bearing our sins in His own body on the tree"; His outpoured blood was the evidence of the completed sacrifice. There would be no efficacy in the death of one man for another. That is why the root of our faith, John says, lies in the fact of the incarnation, "God manifest in the flesh"; so that this was God in human form, the source and upholder of the human race, being "the propitiation for our sins" in His death. The resurrection was the evidence that the atonement was so complete that all consciousness of sin and separation had disappeared for ever, and we who believe are "justified" (Rom. 4:25), legally pronounced as like the risen Christ Himself with "no stain on our character". Forgiveness would not be enough, because though forgiven we remember what we did. Justification means we are as if the thing never happened.

Yet the blood of Christ shed for our sins would not be enough, if Christ crucified and risen was not the means of a total human revolution, the change of gods in the centre of our personality—from occupation by the spirit of error to occupation by the Spirit of truth (1 John 4:6). To have the consequences of a permanent condition of being law-breakers, a life in hell, removed by "the precious blood of Christ", would not be enough if we humans remained possessed and continually motivated by this spirit of error. Only if there is a change of inner indwelling God, and thus change of motivation, can there be this full deliverance. And this Paul revealed to us as having been revealed to him, particularly in his Romans and Galatians letters. When Christ died, this was the human race on that cross, for He was our representative. So in that identification He was in God's sight "made sin". Sin is character of the sin-spirit which produces the sins, and the human race has this spirit within it. Then in His death, it is said "He died unto sin", for death separates body from spirit, and this separated all who believe from that false god. His burial (still representing all of us "buried with Him") indicated that there was a dead body in the tomb with no spirit. The resurrection (still we risen with Him) was the entry and union of the Spirit of God with the dead body which represented the human race. And here was the change of gods, by the grace of God, completed for all of us who exercise our free capacity of choice in receiving, recognizing and affirming our union with Him.

Now our choice changes, when through repentance (change of mind) we are ready to discard our old faith in our self-life, recognize our wrong-doings, and transfer our choice of faith to salvation through Christ. What we take, takes us. We take Jesus, He takes us; and the consequence is God's love shed abroad in our hearts. We begin, compulsively, not of duty but by a new dynamic, the tremendous revolution of a human being, the new birth, in which for the first time in our human history we begin to love somebody else more than ourselves. We start by loving Him who died for us. But when we love Him, we also begin to love people, for He is identified with people. But it is not our love. By no means so, because human love can only be self-love. It is God's own love shed abroad in our hearts by His Spirit (Rom. 5:5). We have begun to *be*, not to *have* the eternal love. We have come home, the prodigal to the Father. Only it is an inner spiritual home-coming of which the parable is an outer symbol. Our home-coming is a union of spirit with Spirit. We have become branches of the Vine, one entity, one person as Head and body make a person; and as a branch is the spontaneous expression of the tree-life, we are the tree in one of its local forms.

This is what the creation of man in the image of God meant—that we should be little Christs, Jesus in human form. This is why God was manifest in the flesh in Jesus—that the meaning of manhood might be completely seen in Him and then become possible through His atoning work.

That earlier second experience I had in the Congo is what establishes us in the permanent awareness of this unity. I have sought earlier to explain a little of what it meant, but it is important enough to warrant a little repetition. At our new birth we find by painful experience that however anxious we are to be what we should be, the redeemed human self can never by itself rise above its human selfhood. We learn the hard way, by what we call "the wilderness experience", not just the guilt of not having been what we should but the helplessness of not being able to be what we should be, and the great liberation of discovering that we are not *meant* to be different; we cut the words "ought to" (Rom. 7) out of our vocabulary! We have this second collapse—that the self will never be more than a container of the Divine Self: the self will not change, and will not become better and is not meant to, but contains the One who is all change.

We are then conditioned to see the fact of the eternal unity, our humanity the containers of His deity: He the all, not making us something different, not giving us love or power or peace or wisdom, but Himself being all that in us; He through the unity manifesting Himself in all these characteristics of the One God by us, so that it is the fruit of the

Spirit which is love, joy, peace and the rest in Galatians 5:22, 23, and not our human fruitage. So we come home. This second crisis of faith affirms this relationship, and what we take takes us: and the Spirit in His own way and time bears witness with our spirits that He and I are a unity.

Now we live the normal human life. We accept ourselves for He has accepted us; and when we accept instead of reject ourselves, we accept others instead of rejecting them. We just are ourselves, that's all; for we *are* the will of God, and we *are* the light of the world, and we *are* as He is in this world. And we are free. We dare to be ourselves, instead of the old watchful fear of constant failure, because in this unity we are held, not we hold Him; and we leave Him to do the holding while we live our normal lives. We leave Him to mind His own business, and we are His business.

Life has fewer strains, battles and problems—for a very good reason. As local expressions of God, and He is love, we are love in action. We are in a world, and are a part of it, which is torn asunder by the opposite of that love. We see it and feel it and are meant to see and feel. It is only when we have reactions that we are involved in situations. This is the purpose of us being humans. It is not wrong to have a human reaction to people or things. We are meant to; and our human reactions are normally negative—fear, dislike, anxiety, hate, disgust. If we were of the world, we should get caught up by these feelings and know no way of deliverance from them. Now we recognize them as having a purpose, not for ourselves; we are the branches of a Vine which is producing fruit for others; we are the body of the Person who is the Saviour and Intercessor for the world. We have passed on from a Christ for our convenience. He has become that now, fixed and settled. We are now part of a Christ for others. So we take a different point of view in our disturbing situations.

He has put us where indifferent neighbours, blasphemous workmates, disturbing social conditions have their impact on us. We have our family problems, our unsaved loved ones, our church and mission discords, our physical sicknesses, our economic uncertainties. But now they are for a different purpose. They are not for our betterment or further training or sanctification (though they may have some incidental side-effects that way). They are God's ways of revealing Himself to others by us. All life is now an intercession. We accept the unpleasant situations as from God, though apparently sometimes from the devil or man. This is what Paul meant in 2 Corinthians 4:10 by "always bearing about in the body the dying of the Lord Jesus". As Jesus died to Himself at Gethsemane in accepting a death which He wished He could escape, so we die to our desire to resist or refuse what we would like to escape. This is the dying fulfilled in our bodies.

But where there is a dying there is a rising. As we by acceptance die to our hurt selves, we have a consciousness of Him living His life in us. We have a poise, faith, peace, liberty, which hurt self does not have. The life of Jesus is being manifested in our mortal body, and people see something different from the usual way of behaviour in unpleasant circumstances. Then also, being freed from self-pity and self-hurt (though there is the constant hurt), we can now see along with God into something of His purposes in revealing Himself to others by us. We are freed to co-operate by the word of faith that God will do what He plans to do in the specifics He shows us in the situation. We are free to love those whose very antagonisms are proofs that they are really crying out for love, and to give acceptable witness as occasions arise.

The very hurts we so deeply feel become redemptive in stirring us to aroused human reactions which become a springboard for faith—this dying and rising with Him. God can come through to others, where He could not come through unless He first had His dying and rising human agent. So, as Paul summed it up: "Death works in us, but life in you."

What was frustration is now adventure. But we are active agents, not passive recipients. So we go further. Faith is

179

the one way by which we humans involve ourselves actively in anything. We think over a thing, we make a decision that we will do that thing, and then we do it. That is faith—thought, word and deed. A carpenter thinks over what kind of chair he will make (thought). He decides and maybe designs the type he will make (word). He then proceeds to get his wood and tools and makes it (deed). That is faith in action. But note that the decisive moment is the Word. That is why creation was said to be by "The Word", and why all dramatic deliverances and supplies in the Bible records of the men of faith centred in their spoken *word* of faith. Speaking the word for us humans means that we have come out of our inner undecided selves into becoming people of decisive action: "I will do so and so." The deed is really the outward clothing of the word, and proceeds naturally and easily from it. In creation, God as The Father was The Thinker. God as The Son was The Speaker. And from Them proceeded God the Spirit as The Doer.

A human by his faith in action can only go as far as he has human resources to utilize—a carpenter must have his tools and his wood. But we, in God, participate in the eternal resources. It is not our paltry human thinking, human affirming, human action. It is we as being He—He thinking, speaking, acting by us. So now we must watch against that sin of all sins—the sin of unbelief. Unbelief is really negative faith. It is believing the wrong way round, believing human appearances, in the hopelessness of things, in our weakness, in the dark situations of which life is full, producing fear, anxiety, pessimism. Unbelief is faith in the power of evil.

We are to replace negative faith by positive. As "gods" (John 10:34,35) we are to do as Jesus said: Express God's faith and "say" to our mountains "Be thou removed". We are to *speak* the words of faith which are creative and reproductive, just because it is the word which is the decisive committal. Not asking for a thing, but declaring it as done. Calling "the things that be not as though they were". As we do this, the Spirit moves to transmute the faith into substance, because it has all along not been our human faith or human word, nor will it be our human deed. Having the mind of Christ, we take it that the direction of our thoughts and desires is His, He working in us to will of His good pleasure. Speaking the word of faith, we boldly say it is He speaking it by us; it is not we having faith in God, but having and expressing the faith of God (according to the correct marginal translation of Mark 11:22). He who gave the thought and constrained us to speak the word, does the deed.

That may include Him saying to us, "Now, I'll do it by you." Certainly. A missionary says yes to that. It may take four or forty years. Jesus fulfilled His faith by the offering of His body to be crucified, in faith for the resurrection. He never saw the outcome of His faith this side of the grave.

Faith is the whole man in action: therefore it involves our bodies, and there is a sense in which we answer our own prayers. "It all depends on God and it all depends on me" has truth in it. That is the faith James speaks of, which without works is dead: "I will show thee my faith by my works." Having spoken the word of faith, we expect to be involved to any limit in fulfilling it. Salvation was by the offering of the *body* of Jesus. If love belongs to need, and we are an expression of that eternal love, then it will involve our time, our money, our physical labours, our homes, our earthly security.

There is a law, a principle at work in this, to which Jesus referred when He said, "Except a corn of wheat fall into the ground and die, it abideth alone, but if it die, it bringeth forth much fruit." Whatever form it may assume, this we take for granted—that the whole of us will be involved. Not by self-effort, not by pressing ourselves to get into action, but we shall find ourselves compelled: "the love of Christ constraineth me". We have to, and love to, right in the midst of the cost of it. For the joy set before us, we too endure our cross. Faith works by love in action. Yet through it all we know it is not our efforts, our so-called sacrifices, which

181

bring the results. It is the faith which even through years of waiting has already declared the outcome.

This I understand to be the meaning of life and the adventure of loving. It is all inclusive, because I see the devil only as God's agent; there is no permissive but only directive will of God. He works all things after the counsel of His own will, and it is the good pleasure of His will. He enjoys it, and so do we by faith. So there is a wholeness to being: no second causes. Even where the enemy, operating through the perverted freewill of man, appears strong and dominant, we see him under God's directive control, already defeated at the cross, and we with the Victor "far above all". We are the privileged ones to be the channels of faith and love through our self-giving, by which the victory will be visibly manifested. The shout of a king is among us.

This is a brief outline, which I have sought to expand to the fullest of my understanding in those last two books, *God Unlimited* and *The Spontaneous You*. It is this which has given me a broad base to a faith with understanding. In that critical year, while shaken by my questioning of God, even when going through it, I came to one decision. I had so known and loved the Lord and He had been so real to me through the past twenty years, that I said to myself, "If God is an illusion, He is so wonderful and so satisfies all I can conceive He should be, that if He is the great illusion, I will remain a little illusion along with Him."

But by the end of a year the mist had cleared. I can't exactly say how except that it was while I was reading John of the Cross's *Ascent of Mount Carmel*; and the result has been worth all the agony of that year. The awareness of the unity became a fixture which has never varied since. I think I would say that in the earlier Congo "second experience", Christ in me became a permanent reality: in this one, I in Christ became the permanency: the recognition of me (and all the redeemed) being a part of the One, and functioning each in our local situation as He Himself in a branch form. We are in the same relationship to Him who is the whole, as any workman is to his source material, in the sense that God puts Himself at one's disposal. It is up to us to mould the material into the particular product of our choosing. In this sense God called Moses a god to Pharaoh and a god to Aaron, and Jesus commented on the fact as an inspired word of Scripture that we are gods "to whom the word of God has come", as I have already mentioned. This is the ascended life. Having ourselves been joined to Christ in death and resurrection for our own deliverance and union, we now exercise the authority of a royal priest seated with Him in His royal high priesthood and exercising our priesthood on earth by the operation of a faith which works by love. The permanency of the sense of exaltation, the changeless inner light, the awareness at all times and any moment of the familiarity of being one, so that it is not really I but He, the given fact of a forgiveness and cleansing which preceded any sins by two thousand years, the ability to speak the word of faith on any situation: I cannot say how these have become facts of experience since coming out of that tunnel, but they have.

But I still have to emphasize, even though I cannot make it plain to others, that there has been for me a vital difference between the second experience of discovering Christ living in me, and this third revelation of Christ all in all. The second experience left gaps where I did not yet see Him in everything everywhere, and all a form of Him, whether negatively of Him in wrath as consuming fire, or positively of Him in grace as light; and so there were separations, and callings on Him to be this or do that, in place of affirmings that He is in fullness of His action everywhere, and specifically through my (His) faith in local situations; and thus the constant use of the word of faith which Jesus used and told us to use (Mark 11:22,23), and all the men of faith of the Bible used in their exploits of faith or endurance. Before, that gap had to be bridged on each occasion by outreachings of faith. Now, there is no gap except in momentary human reactions, and therefore only a constant reaffirmation. And to be settled into this union which is a unity, I had to go through a "dark night of the soul" which affected no outward things, but the very inward vitals of my "I and Thou" consciousness.

CONVICTIONS ABOUT WAR

During World War II, on the day that Prime Minister Chamberlain declared war, and the sirens were sounding for the first time, we gathered at our Headquarters and took our usual line—that man's frustrations are God's opportunities for faith. Therefore we should look for God to do what was impossible to man. In war days we could not normally expect increase of recruits, or of finance, or of the opening of new fields. So we asked the Lord to give us all these three, so that the Gospel could continue to go out to the world, no matter what appeared to be against it. And God did. Recruits increased by two hundred, finance was doubled and two new fields were entered.

We had also asked that none of our headquarter buildings would be lost to us by bombing, and they were all preserved, and all lives, though not without some heavy damage. One buzz-bomb fell next door and destroyed several houses with some loss of life. Our No. 17, nearest to the explosion, was so shaken and the furniture and fittings so smashed that we only just came within the limits in which the authorities assess a house worth repairing. But they did repair it. The hostel, built with steel girders, was heavily shaken but withstood the shock. All the household, about twenty, were sleeping in rows on mattresses in the dining-room when the bomb fell. I was away, but Pauline got slightly hurt. She said she could always tell when a buzz-bomb was coming because our little Aberdeen terrier with his keen hearing would jump up and fly for cover before we could hear anything.

Another bomb which fell near by so shook the two houses on the opposite side of the road, of which the W.E.C. owned one, that the next-door neighbours fled and never returned, and we were able to buy the house for very little. But all the houses were so shaken and damaged by the constant bombing that it has been a marvellous provision from the Lord that the County Council have not only taken these somewhat rickety buildings off us but so compensated us that we could move into the magnificent new Bulstrode headquarters, too far out of London to have been shaken by the bombing.

I was never free from fear during the constant bombing raids, night after night for one period. I think I was much more consciously fearful in World War II than in World War I. I had not yet learned, as I have now, that fear is not wrong but natural, and the answer is to recognize and accept the fear, not feel guilty or cowardly because of it, but go ahead reckoning as ever on God's underlying faithfulness.

My own attitude to a Christian's involvement in war has been through several different phases until I have come out to what seems to me a right and Scriptural position.

I started in World War I with just the thoughtless enthusiasm of a young man, I think mainly for the attraction of fighting and getting to the front line, also with a sense of it being the obvious thing to be in with my country in its war involvements. From 1930 onwards I gradually changed my views and could not reconcile fighting and killing and the brutalities of war with the Christian loving all men including his enemies. Yet I never felt I had touched bottom in this. Something was missing, just from the fact that in World War II I was enjoying freedom in my country from Nazism and Fascism, because my countrymen were shedding their blood to maintain it, and because there are police and law courts to preserve order; and freedom in the U.S.A., when I came to live here, because their young men had given their lives for the same cause, and were now in Vietnam, and in all Cold War re-armaments, preserving freedom for us from slavery under Communism. How could I reconcile this with unwillingness as a Christian to share in the price that was being paid in human blood to maintain this?

I found my answer and it satisfies me, when I saw clearly that the Bible divides the human race into two categories—the unredeemed and the redeemed. The unredeemed, all of us by nature until born again, are fundamentally self-regarding and self-seeking; we are not under the inner control of the law of God until it becomes written in our hearts by the Holy Spirit. Therefore we are controlled by an outer law administered by governments, police, law courts and ultimately armies. The law is for the lawless, says Paul, and "the powers that be" are ordained of God, and a ruler is a minister of God and "beareth not the sword in vain", for he "is an avenger to execute wrath upon him that doeth evil".

This also for me explains God's commands in the Old Testament which are often questioned—to destroy the enemies of Israel, whole nations including women and children. This is not a question of individual vengeance or murder. Jesus makes plain that murder issues from the heart. But when individuals or nations are opposing the laws necessary for the maintenance of social order and safety or national existence, then it is God's will and our necessity to use force of arms or of arrest and the law courts. That is on a national or international level, and I am a member of a nation.

On an individual level, if I am a child of God and His Spirit of love indwells me, then I am to seek the best way I can to overcome evil with good, and to do good to those that hate me. I am to turn the other cheek, which means I am less concerned about whether he gives me another blow, because I am more concerned about how I can help heal the bitter spirit which motivated the first blow.

But even then there are problems, so soon as it is not just my individual self. If I am an executive in a firm, I cannot permit dishonesty to continue which does not just hurt me but the firm. If a loved one is being attacked, I cannot stand by, when it is not just I being hurt who might take it for Christ's sake, but someone else. I must go to their defence.

That is how I see it, and therefore for myself justify and benefit by the internal disciplines of my country and external involvements of war. I know there are the problems of, Is my country the aggressor or defender? Each side claims God on his side, and God is on the side of all. But I can only hope my country has the greater justification for being at war; and God, the judge of all, appealed to by both sides, will give victory to the more right of the two. I believe He has done this through history—the Spanish Armada, the Napoleonic wars, the American Revolution, World Wars I and II; and if I am God's man and on the losing side, as in Germany under Hitler, He is still my God and my nation's God, but I can see and accept the justice of God's judgements.

And when a nation with a Christian background does go to war, it is good and right if, after peace has been declared, it manifests no hatred or vengeance, but assists in the up-building of the defeated nation, as the U.S.A. has so magnificently done in restoring prosperity to West Germany and Japan.

So I see us Christians living on two levels—with certain obligations to our nation and the world on the law level; yet my real life and obligation being on the grace level in living the Christ-life on the standards of the Sermon on the Mount.

THE NEW WORLD OF THE U.S.A.

The final, at least I suppose it is final, move of our lives has been to the U.S.A. We came as a family in 1957. The immediate purpose was, in addition to being International Secretary of W.E.C., to act for a time as North American Secretary. This I did, though it was never my niche and I was glad to turn it over to a successor, Elwin Palmer, whom the staff recently elected. I remained as International Secretary till 1965 when, in the triennial election at which all leaders are re-elected or changed, being now seventy, I resigned and nominated the one I was sure was God's man and would be approved by all, Len Moules.

Len is one of the Smith–Moules dynasty who seem to populate W.E.C., as I have already mentioned, from that small Acton Lane Mission Hall in London. Len and Iris were pioneers on the Tibetan border, the film of his escapades in seeking out the Tibetans, *Three Miles High*, drawing big crowds in England. In war days Len became a major in the

British Army, serving with the Desert Rats, the famous desert army under Field-Marshal Montgomery who broke the back of Rommel's advance on Egypt. Spiritually and physically matured as he was, after being British Headquarters leader for five years, it is like a crowning blessing on my W.E.C. years, that in Len Moules God has provided such a successor. Of course the jokers remark that at least we approach the standard of Isaiah, "Fear not, thou worm Jacob", when it is a mole following a grub.

At the close of such an era in Pauline's and my life, 1931 to 1965, I can only say, and I hope it is not deluded boasting, that I have a great sense of thankfulness. Ours has not been the difficult task. C. T. Studd under God gave us our objective and foundations. Ours has been to build on these foundations; and with such standards as these—sacrifice, faith, holiness and fellowship—we do not have those offering to join us who want an easier way. So it has been a matter of guiding and encouraging in the opening of new fields and home-bases, ours the background job, the real soldiers in the fighting lines. So our joy is simple—but all we could wish for—that the Lord's work through the Lord's servants goes right on, to the Lord's appointed end, that "the world through Him might be saved".

For our personal needs, once again what can we say but that God stepped in? We should not have wished to occupy room with our family in the main headquarters building in Fort Washington. Some twenty-five years ago Mrs. Henry Woods of Atlantic City, who dedicated her time and substance to spreading revival literature under the title of The Worldwide Revival Prayer Movement, was looking for a book which she felt could challenge students to a whole-hearted commitment to Christ. She picked up *C. T. Studd* in a library, and we had a letter in London asking if she could cross the Atlantic and see us with a view to publishing a special student gift edition. She came, and Pauline and I met this stately lady, who we felt was a typical example of the best of Americans, in the Russell Hotel. But having talked with us, not only did she suggest the edition but that if I would come over with a helper to organize she would open her files of ten thousand evangelical addresses from which I could arrange some deputation tours.

I went with Fred Anthony and that was the start of our open door into the U.S.A. Mrs. Woods published twenty thousand *C. T. Studds,* and I still continually meet ministers who tell me how this book somehow got to them in their student days and set them on fire. Mrs. Woods continued as our close friend; and then one day, in 1955 while I was in U.S.A. but Pauline and the family still in England, she said the Lord had told her that, if Pauline would come, she was to give us her house when she died. She lived till over ninety, but then in her will, with a generous gift to the mission, she left her house to the mission for the Grubb family as long as they would need it.

We sold her house. Though a big one, being old, the price we received was $12,000. On inquiry from a Christian builder who offered to build for us, our friend Fred Davis, we found that, if we built on W.E.C. or C.L.C. ground, and thus did not have to buy the land, a house such as we needed with four bedrooms would cost around $20,000. So as God was so obviously leading, we went forward. The C.L.C. very kindly gave us a portion of land, so that the building is C.L.C. property, though ours for our lives. But the town permission to build was unaccountably delayed, and it looked as if there was a real hold-up. Not so. It was God's way for the bigger provision.

An old friend, a retired director of a chain of supermarkets, Mr. Fred Heaney, often visited us. He was concerned at Pauline not being able to move and kept inquiring about this permit. When we heard it had come, he asked permission to be present when the final contract was signed with Mr. Davis. But $12,000 is not $20,000! However, when money was mentioned, Mr. Heaney kind of brushed it aside and said we could leave that. Along came cheques of $1,000, $2,000, $3,000, from him, from his son Norman who had been a close friend of mine for years and from someone else anonymous. And when the house, beautifully built, was finished and Mr. Davis brought the bill, he said that for the Lord's sake he was cutting off his normal profit, so that the amount was $18,000, exactly what the Lord had sent.

How we have enjoyed our home, and continually thank God for each of these who so ministered to us. The building was such a finished job that there just have not been problems, as there often are with the way some new houses are constructed.

This house was also another evidence to us that you can't outgive God. We held the deeds of No. 17 Highland Road in London, C. T. Studd's original home which became the first unit of W.E.C. headquarters in London. When we left for the U.S.A., we left everything behind in the way of furnishings, except personal effects, for the next W.E.C. occupants, and were glad it became the home of Len and Iris Moules. When the order came for the removal of W.E.C. from its old headquarters, and they were awaiting the Council assessment for buying this new place, we felt it right to hand over the deeds of No. 17 so that the whole was mission property. Now here when our time of need comes, God steps in and not only is this lovely home provided but also all the furnishings necessary.

OUR CHILDREN

Pauline and I had three children after our first-born Noel had died in the Congo: Paul born 1924, Priscilla in 1925 and Daniel in 1927. We had more home life together than might appear as I have talked of all our mission activities. No. 17 Highland Road was our home from 1928 up to our coming to the U.S.A. in 1957. As soldiers of Jesus, we expected many absences from each other and had them with many journeyings around Britain and a number of foreign tours. But we had our family life with romps around the house, cricket in the garden and family games on winter nights.

We also had wonderful summer holidays. Our friends, Mr.

and Mrs. Fremlin, sent us year after year for a month to a farm on the Scottish moors with gorgeous farmhouse meals and out all day on the heather-clad moors, by the tumbling mountain burns, and swimming in the pools. They were lovely times. During World War II days we were given a beautiful home on the Devon moors in the west of England, one of the houses of Dame Violet Wills who lived near by and whom we came to know through Alfred and Edith Buxton. It stood in its own grounds, which her gardener looked after, with a long drive up to it. She offered to give it to us for a permanency, but though kind of her, our calling was not to the depths of the country. Here again we had picnics out by the old stone quarries which provided climbing for the children and explorations in the bracken-covered moors. She also had a tennis court, which was most welcome. During these vacation periods we always had time for a period in the mornings when we could relax as a family and not just read a Scripture or two but get down together to what the Christian life means; and the children were quick enough to enter in and talk things over.

One can't say much about the present generation because they have to live with Dad and Mum reminiscences, while we pass on! Our eldest son Paul went to school at Dulwich College. He married young, but his wife left him. As they had already been living in an apartment in our home, we took the children of their marriage. They never saw their mother again.

This was a major decision of our middle lives and totally altered life for Pauline. It meant starting again as grandparents to bring up two children, Sandra then aged three-and-a-half and Nicholas aged one-and-a-half, to whom Pauline has given herself as to our own children. We took this to be the Lord's way, so once again she has stayed these years in the home, while I travelled. Paul accepted Christ as a boy, but has not continued in the Christian life. He has recently married again and works in a men's club in the west end of London. The Judge in London was willing to give us guardianship over the two children and let us take them to the U.S.A., because Priscilla our daughter as the in-between generation was coming with us.

She is still with us, having given these years to be with her mother and the children. She gave her life to Christ as a schoolgirl, starting a Christian group in the girls' school, Westonbirt, of which my sister was Principal and who made it possible for her to go there.

Daniel, our youngest, was disturbed in his education through the outbreak of World War II and the London bombing. We had friends in Wayne, Pennsylvania, who have become like a second family to us: Mrs. Elmore, now with the Lord, her daughter Rachael, her son Robert who has a national name as an organist and composer, and a lady doctor, Dr. Mabel Jackson, who helps many by a special treatment on circulation, but even more by showing them how to grasp what the Lord can do for them through faith. These four took Dan into their home and made him like their own son. They so helped him with their love, specially through Dr. Jackson's treatment, that he began an education which took him through King's College, Wheaton College, Duke University and finally to the University of Michigan, one of the great universities of the U.S.A., where he gained his Ph.D. in English literature. When we went to the graduation ceremony, he told us that his success was due to "God's faithfulness". Now as associate professor in the Indiana University of Western Pennsylvania, with his wife Rosemary and little son Danny, his witness to Christ is the main aim of his life.

A marriage in the Lord is a wonderful thing, where from the beginning there is a fundamental harmony in outlook centred in Christ. As I have already said, Pauline and I have had that by God's goodness these forty-nine years. Could I be more glad and thankful for anything than this? I am glad we thrashed out any possible basic differences before we married. Husband and wife are so wonderfully complementary to each other. What a wife in Pauline God gave a volatile Irishman. She has had the stability and reliability I would not have by nature. Of course we battle things through, argue, differ, seek God's mind together and I often do say negative things to her and am sharp and hard with her. But probably it has been good for her also to have a go-getter husband, never satisfied with the status quo. The hare and the tortoise; but remember who won the race. She has been wonderful in her readiness to let me go so much on these journeyings she has not been able to take with me, first because of our own little family, and then because of the grandchildren. It has always cost us and still does, just about the one sacrifice we have been able to make for the Lord.

But my failings as a father have been many. Each of us in the Lord's service has to go the way we seem pressed into by Him. For me it has been the fulfilment of my life's calling to the mission fields; but I think this had had an adverse effect on the children. As I have said, Pauline and I accepted our commission from God from the time of our marriage, so that it has been a gladly accepted sacrifice of much home life, though always costly to both of us. No one could have been a more devoted mother than she, and the children and two grandchildren we have brought up deeply know that. But we haven't put enough glory into God's call and way of life in W.E.C. to make it attractive to them as it has been to us. My relationship with my eldest son has always been easy, we seem to have a natural affinity and enjoy the rare times now when we can be together. But, of course, to me the sorrow is that the day has not yet come when God has taken over his life; though it will come. My youngest son and I did not hit it off during his teenage years. I had somehow put a fear of me into him. This has totally changed in adult years and our love and fellowship is the closest, most particularly because we love to talk together as deeply as we know how on the things of the Spirit. I think a break came when I confessed to him one day when my attitudes and actions had not been right towards him. My daughter has a deep love for her mother, and has really given her life to remaining with her in the upbringing of the two grand-children. She loves the Lord too, but it has been the other way round with her. Our link was close in her younger days, we used to love walks together; but I have often spoilt it in later years by seeking to put pressure on her during the years in which she has lived in a more retiring way, instead of leaving God to take her His way in His time, which He surely is doing.

I do not say I could have gone any other way than we have gone. What can you do when you are captured and driven? But I do see that the family have paid a price so that the Gospel could get to more peoples in the world; and God will not be unmindful of that in their lives and needs. George Muller always said his daughter Lydia had a permanent claim on God because her father had based his life on God's faithfulness, and we say the same to our children.

WIDENING OUTREACHES OF THE SPIRIT

Increasingly in these U.S.A. years, I have been widening my contacts with people. The winds of God are blowing widely these days, and by no means confined to our own selected areas. We conservative evangelicals are in danger of being ghettos, walling ourselves in and keeping others out. I believe we are in a new and thrilling era of the outreaches of the Spirit. A half-century ago, when I was at Cambridge, we evangelical Bible-believers had our backs to the wall; the liberals seemed to hold the field, and we took our stand against encroaching modernism by founding our Bible and Christ-centred associations, churches, missions. I believe we were right, and I could not to this day throw in my lot for a life's ministry except with those who held the same fundamentals.

But I also thankfully recognize that great ferments have been at work in the whole church of Christ throughout its whole spectrum: the shocks of two world wars; the menace of atheistic communism, the first time atheism has proclaimed itself as a rival faith; the blatant secularism, and dissatis-faction with establishment Christianity; the challenge brought

194

to the ranks of liberal theology by Karl Barth, Emil Brunner and the like. For though these men do not go all the way with us in Biblical orthodoxy, yet by combining scholarship with a prophetic authority they have recalled thousands, who would not listen to an old-line fundamentalist, to the plain observable and Biblical facts of the fall of man, the necessity of redemption, the uniqueness of Christ as Saviour, Lord, and God, and the reality of regeneration.

When I first read Karl Barth's *Römerbrief*, his commentary on the Epistle to the Romans, it was to me like the finding of hidden treasure. I had read nothing equal to it on Romans, and it led me to a greater than Barth, who had much influenced him—Søren Kierkegaard. On his writings I continually feed with his combination of a massive intellect, a passionate search for the truth, a pulverizing of man-made self-upbuilding philosophies. He almost lassoes his readers and drags them to the edge of the impassable gulf between God and man, and shuts them in to the only bridge of the "absurdity of faith" in a God manifested in the flesh by His atoning act.

Through these underminings of the old liberal delusion of a world getting better and better, and man on the road to universal self-improvement, supposedly under the inspiration of the good example of "the Jesus of history", has now come bursting forth the floods of an honest reappraisal of the Christian church in our generation, its message, its effectiveness, its forms of organization and worship. That which needs to be shaken is being shaken, and those who say that in a generation or two the outward church will not be recognizable in comparison to the outward church of today may be right. The challenges come in some forms and by some voices with whom we have often to disagree, but their very reception shows they are touching a chord. We would do well to mark this and profit by it. Two unimaginable outbreaks are evidence of this: at one end of the pole the outbreak of the charismatic gifts, particularly tongues, in the church world-wide from Rome to the Bible churches; at the other, the shakings going on within Rome itself, an honest, fearless, outspoken re-appraisal of the claims of Rome by Roman Catholics themselves, priests and laity, to be the Christian faith which conforms to Bible revelation. World-shaking.

As far as Rome is concerned, I don't believe there is one of my generation who could have dreamt of such a thing happening in that apparently unassailable monolith. To any who know the facts, especially to many of us who are in living contact with priests, nuns and laity eager for simple fellowship in Christ, it is absurd to put our heads in the sand and say it is all a subtle racket to get us back into Rome. It isn't. It is a breath of God. Of course, there is the stiff opposition of the right wing in Rome, the Curia and others. Have not we conservatives an equally stiff right wing? I am not saying that the basic dogmas of Rome are changed or that there is at present a serious attempt to change them. But I do say there are shakings and crumblings—and walls have to begin falling apart before the foundations are reached.

The important consequence, at least to me, is that I should drop my past prejudices. I have lived with the immediate suspicion of a black-robed priest or nun as the enemy. I have not had an attitude of charity or anywhere near readiness to think that we might seek and find a basis for a mutual faith in Christ. But I am challenged now to reach out a hand to hands reached out to us.

I have already mentioned the charismatic gifts. I cannot go with so many evangelicals in denouncing these gifts either as Satanic, or fleshly, or in taking the position, with no Scriptural authority, that gifts ceased with the early church. What weaker argument could there be than to quote 1 Corinthians 13:8, "Whether there be tongues, they shall cease", when the same verse says, "whether there be knowledge, it shall vanish away"? We haven't come quite there yet! Anyone who mixes, as I do, in wide enough circles to meet with dozens of Christians from all kinds of denominational backgrounds, into whose lives there has obviously come, through

196

receiving this gift of tongues, a new dimension of warmth, love of Christ, love of people, zeal to witness, knows that it is absurd and indeed blasphemous to call this Satanic. Is warmth, praise, even if with a loud voice, raising of hands, combined with vocal praying, fleshly, any more than coldness, formality, deadness, inability to pray or witness? The fact that zeal takes some of those who have these gifts too far in seeking to urge others to have them, or in claiming them to be the definitive evidence of receiving the Holy Spirit, makes them sometimes a divisive element among us, and I regret that; but it does not give me the right to condemn the gift wholesale; nor do I see why I should contribute to the divisiveness by demanding their excommunication, which is only the reverse form of their demanding that I must have this gift. No, I prefer to see all these as marvellous signs at the polar opposites of the Christian church, of the present-day outpourings of the Spirit.

What I find from all this is a new openness among Christians of all persuasions to forget their local loyalties and seek together the answers to genuine living. I think that this was the genius of the Spirit in Billy Graham that he risked (and got) the disapprobation of some fundamentalists in opening the doors of co-operation widely to any Christians who would join him in getting the Gospel to the unchurched. The enormous result has been that he has really reached the world as no one else ever has, on every level of society and race; whereas, if he had confined his preaching just to those who held the same fundamentals as he holds, he would only be reaching his own sort.

I think this was the warning of the prophet to Israel, that they had better not think they had a corner on truth and the grace of God: if they were the married wife, they would see that the barren woman would have the children.

MODERN MOVEMENTS OF THE SPIRIT

My own experiences have been largely with what is known as "Faith at Work" in the U.S.A. It is not a movement or society, but a fellowship with no membership, which believes that this is the day for team-work and small groups as the most living expression of Christ's church in action; and we seek to link in with churches of all kinds to help the ministers and congregations in this style of fellowship living and witness. It has spread rapidly over the U.S.A. and Canada these past fifteen years, and is beginning to make inroads into Britain and other countries.

Its main activity is area conferences. There were about twenty-five of these last year. Usually we can't get the numbers in. We take a hotel in a main city, and if it can hold four hundred, there are another two hundred applicants we have to turn down. We are a family together, calling each other by our first names, with an atmosphere of freedom, love and acceptance of each other. No questions asked, and no shock when some are smokers, or others may have what some might call a worldly appearance. But there is no doubt about the sole aim of the weekends. The team meets a day before, maybe thirty or forty, sharing up-to-date news of what the Lord is doing in their own lives, praying and seeking God's pattern for the public meetings. There are never preachments, but a sharing of experiences of the changes Christ has brought. The heart-beat of the conferences are the talk-it-over groups, when the whole company is divided into groups of about ten, with a man and woman (not husband and wife) "moderating", to keep it from going off into tangents. These meet all over the hotel or conference centre. Folks introduce themselves and are soon deep in something which someone raises. The same groups meet three times during the weekend. There is also a daily Bible hour; and one afternoon is for workshops, when a number of subjects are offered for serious study together, and people choose which they wish to attend. Back home many catch the vision of groups in their home churches. Many ministers come, and there are also special clergy conferences.

I was introduced to Faith at Work before it was actually called that, some fifteen years ago. Irving Harris, who has been my intimate friend since then, used to meet with a group in the fellowship centre attached to Sam Shoemaker's Episcopal Church in New York. I was immediately attracted by the warmth and acceptance of that little group. It included the friend of all of us, the red-cap (Negro railway porter) at Grand Central Station, Ralston Young, whose story had been published in *Reader's Digest*. My own contribution on their board, with Bruce Larson the Executive Secretary and the others, has been my conviction that God has a work through F.A.W. both nation-wide and world-wide.

When we were at first concentrated in eastern U.S.A., I urged extension to the West Coast, knowing from my own tours the throbbing and expanding life of California and the Northwest. F.A.W. has now spread throughout the West. Then in the Southern States, where I have always felt so much at home (perhaps the Southerners are more like the British in their culture), a society couple from Montgomery, the capital of Alabama, zoomed up like a rocket after God had got hold of them—Sidney and Louise Mohr. I challenged her to get going through the south, and get going she did, until there are now conferences in every state of this conservative south, and crowded ones too.

Then came England. There seemed an open door into which Irving Harris stepped by several visits, I joining him on one of them. A U.S.A. team who wondered how they would be received, found the "reserved" British wide open, and now a British team is just getting going, which is already beginning to spread across the country and meet great needs, including Douglas Greenfield from York, Rona Bradley, Murray and Oda Webb-Peploe and others.

Another particular friend and interest has been Abram Vereide and the International Christian Leadership which he founded. For some reason unknown to me, about twenty years ago he sought me out when I was visiting the West Coast, where he was then living in Seattle and asked me to speak to a small breakfast group. At that time I was used to moving in my own more closed circle and was not used to these folks who obviously came from a different background; and one of my evangelical friends made it worse by warning me Mr. Vereide was too broad in his affiliations. So there I was caught in our negative ghetto trap. It must have been only something of the broad grace of God which led him to contact me again about two years later. That contact has become a life's friendship.

Meanwhile he had taken the great step from his Seattle ministry among immigrants in need (he himself was a Norwegian immigrant) to finding his true calling in reaching the "up and outs". His first break in was among the civic and business leaders of Seattle which was then in the grip of the racketeers. From this he moved on until he established the now nationally known House and Senate weekly prayer groups in the Capitol in Washington, D.C., with his wonderful God-given touch in making friends with the nation's leaders, talking with them of their need of God in their responsibilities and of a personal commitment to Christ.

From these came the start of the Presidential Prayer Breakfasts once a year, attended first by President Eisenhower, then by President Kennedy and by President Johnson. Abram asked me to have a morning devotional meeting in the hotel where the Breakfast would be, an hour before the breakfast, and I have had these for ten years. It is remarkable how men and women (for there is a First Lady's Breakfast at the same time as the men's) crowd in for that period, and seem to gobble up the message on the indwelling Christ.

The breakfasts are unique experiences. On the dais is the President of the U.S.A. with about twenty others—the Vice-President, the Chief Justice, the Leaders of the House and Senate, various Secretaries of State and State Governors. The banquet hall, holding a thousand, is filled with senators and congressmen, leaders of the armed services, judiciary, leaders of business, Negro representations, union executives and so forth. We sit in tables of about twelve. The atmosphere has the warmth of an evangelistic meeting. The army chorus starts with some song like "Sweet Hour of Prayer". There is a word on the purpose of the Breakfast by the chairman, Senator Carlson, prayer, a solo by some noted singer but who also can witness for the Lord. It was remarkable one year to hear Jerome Hines of the Metropolitan Opera, before he sang, say how he had been up in the early morning asking the Lord what to sing, and the Lord had told him he was not there to sing for the President but for the glory of Jesus who was his personal Saviour; and then with his magnificent baritone he sang "Blessed Assurance".

There is a short talk by the Congressman who is responsible for the weekly Congress prayer sessions, and the Senator likewise. There are readings from the Old and New Testament, and then the main speaker, several times Billy Graham, who always makes as plain as can be the need of a personal commitment to Christ. The President himself gives a short word, President Johnson on what prayer means to him and that such an occasion is an annual recognition of the nation being under God.

These Washington breakfasts have now spread over the nation into Governors' Prayer Breakfasts in each State, and many Mayors' breakfasts, a thousand last year, and in foreign countries also, always aiming at the leadership of the nations. I was asked to write Abram's life, which I was able to do with the early accounts he had already briefly written of his early years, and much from our friend Marian Aymar Johnson who has been a strength behind this International Christian Leadership from its beginnings. It was published under the title of *The Modern Viking*. A specially bound copy was prepared for President Kennedy, and Abram took me with him into the room where they gather before going in to the breakfast, Chief Justice Warren, the Vice-President (then Lyndon Johnson) and others awaiting the arrival of the President. I was to present the book to him. Unfortunately, he came late so it had to be given to him afterwards.

I have had some connections, though not so close, with

another movement of the Spirit, widespread in the U.S.A., going under the strange title of Camps Farthest Out. It was founded some years ago by the late Glenn Clark. It holds "camps" in about fifty conference centres or hotels in the various states, with hundreds of "campers" at each. I have been to several. They are looked upon with some suspicion by most evangelicals because they have no defined doctrinal basis, and rumours have got around that some far-out viewpoints, not accepted by the average Bible-believer, such as reincarnation or universalism, have been taught from their platforms. There have been instances of this. I heard one and protested. But it is a definite policy of C.F.O. that they do not advocate such viewpoints, and their interest is not in propagating some unusual or exotic theories, but something far different. Love and prayer are their keynotes.

From my experience, any of us who are more accustomed to the set pattern of our evangelical Bible conferences and who go to one of the "camps", find ourselves engulfed in a warmth of love which campers are not inhibited in expressing, a warmth we can do well to take back to our own circles. But it is no sentimental love, because it finds its expression in the most down-to-earth on-the-spot praying of the prayer of faith. The central activity is the afternoon prayer groups which are for the mention of specific needs, usually (though not compulsorily) accompanied by the one mentioning the need taking a seat in the centre of the group, while the others gather round, lay hands according to the Scriptures and some pray simple prayers of faith.

The emphasis is always simple faith. What we ask, we believe we receive, and the prayers turn to praise. You have a sense that something practical, the needs of a wanderer from Christ, a physical healing, the larger needs of a world, are brought to God on the spot without a lot of peripheral wording, committed to Him, released to Him and thanks given for the answer that is coming. I find it enormously refreshing compared to the standard prayer meeting where a number of people pray general prayers which may or may not include specific needs, but which do not there and then in each separate instance issue in a completed prayer of faith and praise.

Actually from my experience it is a travesty that the idea should have got abroad that C.F.O. teaching and preaching is off-beam. Christ is its centre, His blood, His Spirit, His word, His miracle-working power. They have their own song book which contains a great number of most original little choruses, many new to me, but with the real touch of the Spirit in them. In the Communion Service about twelve at a time kneel round a low table on which in the centre are several large loaves of bread surrounded by bunches of grapes; the bread and wine is passed from one to the other.

Well known among them are Frank Laubach, Starr Daily converted in a prison cell, Tommy Tyson, Roland Brown and one who shone like a star and is now with the Lord—Rufus Moseley, the reporter from Macon, Georgia.

MORE OPEN DOORS TO MORE OPEN HEARTS

After I had felt it right to hand over the leadership of our North American headquarters, though I still remained International Secretary up till 1965, a change came over the overriding interests and objectives of my remaining years. I suppose it was gradual; but more and more I had become settled in my understanding of the meaning of life and the key to living. It had all seemed to fall into place. A big claim, but it had just become that for me. It was like a jig-saw puzzle with the pieces at last in place and the whole picture completed. That completed picture is what I have outlined shortly a few pages back, and sought to put into complete focus in *God Unlimited* and *The Spontaneous You*. I had given a few talks along these lines in one conference centre and someone who had recorded them put them into booklet form under the bold title *The Key to Everything*. Moody Press has printed this and it has gone and still goes in tens of thousands. And I still say that to me it is the key to everything—however presumptuous it may seem to say so.

With this clarification for my own understanding, I began to find hundreds of eager people all over this country who had good evangelical teaching and a born again experience and often a sound understanding of the Scriptures, yet had not, by all means not, found the total key to living.

So I began an expanded ministry. I shall always and for ever have my primary interest where my life roots are, in helping to get the gospel to the whole world, and for me that means through the agencies of the W.E.C. and C.L.C. But I now find open doors and responsive hearts all over the U.S.A. and Canada, and far more than I can take, visiting homes, groups and sometimes churches and conferences, who want to find this key. Where possible, I like three- or four-day sessions when there is time to give in some detail what fills me to the brim with desire to share it. I like it best where we can have an atmosphere of informality, gathered in a circle, and where there is a give and take, an interchange, all learning together from the One Teacher and by no means a group learning from a man. I am not much good at larger public meetings. Having had no training in elocution, my words come pouring out far too fast; and combine that with an English accent, which sounds to them like a foreign tongue, it is hard for my American hearers to get much, at least at first hearing.

In addition to the speaking sessions, maybe because I am older and some have more confidence in opening up the depths of their hearts and problems to an older man, I have a great deal of heart-to-heart correspondence, often with women in their marital problems. There is no greater thrill than to see so many discovering that their sorrows and frustrations are only the Lord's prisons, which shut them up to Him only; and then they find that it is the Lord Himself who is coming to them in the guise of their frustrations, the prison doors open and they are free in the adventure of faith and love.

Sex problems, so much in the public eye these days, and about which we evangelicals have been so hush-hush, are often a cause of frustration within the married life and without; and frank talking leading to a healthier understanding and adjustment is often the key to a new release. How to accept the human as human, without guilt for normal human drives; how to recognize that pleasure is God's gift and blessing which accompanies purpose, but is not a usurper of it. If pleasure replaces purpose as the end in itself, that is corruption leading to hell. If purpose is out front, then pleasure is a happy companion. If we live to eat and the pleasure of eating is the end in itself, we shall soon blow up. If we eat to live, and the necessity of keeping fit is the reason why we eat, then in addition we also thoroughly enjoy the good meal. If sex is for self-gratification, the end is death, as Proverbs makes emphatically clear (chapters 2, 5, 6, 7 and 9). If in the marriage bond it is a token of the total self-giving of the one to the other, then it has the fulfilment Proverbs also speaks of (chapter 5).

And then the greater understanding that, when Freud makes eros the elemental drive of life, he touches a true spot, if he also understood, which he did not, that the capacity for love is the human means for the expression of God loving by us, our passions are the channel for His compassion; and sex itself a river-bed for the streams of God loving all He sends us to love. Then we are free and unafraid. We dare to understand ourselves, accept ourselves and give ourselves in human relationships—to love with His love, responding to that hunger in all to be loved and to love, till they find in us, not one human loving another, but Christ loving them through a human love.

There is no more appealing characteristic of Americans than their warmth and capacity for friendship. I must say it has made life wonderful for Pauline and me these past twelve years. Their hearts and homes are just open. I don't know whether it is so among all Americans, but it certainly is among the Lord's people. But here I am up against a difficulty. I should love to name the families and friends, not just where I have paid a visit, but those whose homes have become home to me, where I often visit, usually at least once a year, and where not only do we have marvellous fellowship ourselves in the things of the Spirit, but, like Cornelius of old, they gather in their friends to hear "all the things that are commanded thee of God". But when I begin to run through their names in my mind, what shall I do?

They are from north to south, from east to west: New England, New York State, Pennsylvania (of course); Washington, D.C., Virginia and West Virginia, North and South Carolina, Tennessee; Georgia, Alabama, Florida; over to the far west in California, Oregon and State of Washington; some, though fewer, in the middle west—Ohio, Indiana, Illinois, Michigan, Minnesota, Kentucky; a few in the middle south—Oklahoma, Kansas, Texas; and that is not mentioning eastern and western Canada in Ontario, Quebec and B.C.

I have left behind my dear friends of years in England, except for exchange of letters and very occasional visits to the Old Country, so I named at least some of them; but these are my present American family among whom we are living, and to whom more are added each year. So probably the best thing is not to attempt names. But it seems there will be no end while I am still given the present abounding health to get around (by all the many convenient means of transport in this country—air, train, bus and car). Like Peter and those with him, how can we be still? "We cannot but speak the things which we have seen and heard"; and always our great aim, and thank God with outspreading results, is that those who hear and see—which are many—then get busy sharing with their neighbours what they have found. The lamp lit in the family home becomes a lighthouse.

I hope by God's continuing grace, it may be true of Pauline and me, as of you, my readers, that having with Paul counted all things but loss that we may win Christ, "and know Him and the power of His resurrection and the fellowship of His sufferings, being made conformable to His death", with Paul also "forgetting those things which are behind and reaching forth unto those things which are before", we shall "press toward the mark for the prize of the high calling of God in Christ Jesus".

INDEX